Politics and Revelation

Māwardī and After

Hanna Mikhail

EDINBURGH UNIVERSITY PRESS

Edinburgh University Press Ltd
22 George Square, Edinburgh

Set in Linotron Trump Medieval
by Koinonia Ltd, Bury, and
printed and bound in Great Britain
at the Alden Press, Oxford

A CIP record for this book is available
from the British Library

ISBN 0 7486 0519 3 (cased)

Contents

Acknowledgements

As hope faded after long years of expectation, the bitter fact of the death of a very special person, who was also a partner, dear friend and companion, had to be faced. The best way of transforming the sorrow of losing Hanna (or Abu Omar) was to keep his memory alive in his writings, which reflect the ideals and goals he cherished and for which he lived. Unfortunately, most of his work was destroyed in the 1982 Israeli invasion of Lebanon, but it seemed most appropriate to publish his PhD dissertation on Māwardī, which embodies Hanna's restless pursuit of deep and comprehensive knowledge as a tool for achieving the noble values of liberation and human progress. Indeed, this was one of the very reasons why such a valuable work of research was not published in book-form a long time ago, for Hanna wanted to develop the ideas in his dissertation as well as to elaborate on the differing perspectives held by himself and his academic supervisor, Dr Nadaf Safran.

Shortly after he began serious revision of the thesis, Hanna tragically disappeared. This was in July 1976, at the height of the civil war in Lebanon. It subsequently became clear that his life had been sacrificed in the struggle for his people and for a free democratic Palestine.

Many people and friends volunteered time and effort to bring this book to completion. My deep gratitude and thanks go to them all. First, my thanks go to the late Sir Hamilton A. R. Gibb – Hanna himself had wanted to acknowledge Sir Hamilton's valuable supervision of the first draft. Very special thanks go to Professor Edward W. Said who, despite his illness, wrote the Preface memorial article, and to Professor Biancamaria Scarcia Amoretti, who was keen to see the book published and who wrote the Foreword. I am grateful to the late Dr Albert Hourani, whose high evaluation of the book was an additional encouragement for its publication; to Professor Ridwan Al-Sayyid, who was kind enough to volunteer to update it; and to Professor Aziz Al-Azmeh, who read the text and the update and was always ready to answer any queries. Thanks are due also to Kamal Bullata, the well-known Palestinian artist, who deserves my full appreciation for kindly volunteering to provide a cover illustration at very short notice.

A number of friends helped me through and were very supportive. To all of them, especially Anna Enayat, Julia Helou and Anne Rodford, go my warm thanks.

Finally, I cannot but express all my love to my two families, the Helous and Mikhails, for their constant support.

Jehan Helou Mikhail
March 1995

Note

The author's text has been updated in some places by Ridwan al-Sayyid. This is indicated in the text by asterisked footnotes and in the endnotes by square brackets around the additional comments.

Preface

EDWARD W. SAID

In the years after the Second World War, approximately forty-nine independent African countries came into existence. India gained its freedom in 1947, Indonesia two years later. Several other former colonial territories in East Asia and in the Arab world followed suit. Only Palestine went against the general current. Its predominantly Arab society was destroyed in 1948 and supplanted by a new Jewish state whose purpose was to settle the territory with incoming Jews from all over the world. Yet Palestine was restored to the historical pattern of decolonization when in the post-1967 period a new nationalist and anti-colonial resistance movement took form, with the Palestine Liberation Organization at its head. Yet, alone among all modern anti-colonial movements, the PLO capitulated to the colonial occupation *before* that occupation had been defeated and forced to leave. This of course has been called a 'compromise', as embodied in the Oslo Declaration of Principles and the subsequent Cairo and Paris agreements, but the various euphemisms do little to conceal what on the Palestinian side was in effect a massive abandonment of principles, the main currents of Palestinian history, and national goals. Every conceivable abridgement of Palestinian self-determination was accepted as part of 'limited self-rule', an arrangement which leaves Israel in charge not only of the exits and entrances to Gaza and Jericho, but also of fifty per cent of Gaza itself, and most of the West Bank, where the combination of settlements and roads ensures that Palestinian autonomy will take place in half a dozen separated cantons (or ghettos).

Once again, the extent of a now official Palestinian amnesia was demonstrated in Yasser Arafat's speech in Cairo on 4 May 1994. He spoke of Palestinian sacrifices 'for peace', as if it were a well-known fact that the Palestinian struggle was really not about self-determination and rights but about getting the dubious achievements of the Gaza–Jericho Accord. Whereas Yitzhak Rabin spoke about Israeli blood and Arab terror, rendered in his customary repertory of distorted, preposterous lies and half-truths that portrayed the Palestinian victims as the aggressors, Arafat referred passively to his people as 'living on their land for the entirety of their history' – as if they had never been dispossessed, dispersed, killed, imprisoned and militarily occupied by the very Israeli leaders he was now publicly embracing.

I have always been in favour both of reconciliation and negotiation between Arabs and Jews as equals in Palestine, but not at the expense only of the Palestinian people. Why should we be required not only to give up what we have lost to military occupation and pillage but in addition to apologize for having made any claims in the first place? Yet the worst aspect of both the Cairo and Paris agreements (on economic relationships with Israel) makes Israel a senior partner in what goes on within the domain of Palestinian 'autonomy': Israel is part of the economic arrangements, Israel must approve Palestinian laws and appointments, Israel has been given extraterritorial privileges for its settlers and military. Thus a new and, in my opinion, crippling dependency for Palestine has been institutionalized and is now set to unfold, with an easily foreseen set of extremely unpromising circumstances as the result. No wonder the PLO now seems so hesitant and unready to take up the autonomy it so unwisely agreed to.

Although the Palestinian people as a whole will continue to suffer under the new dispensation, it is not true that all will suffer equally. If Israel has emerged as a victor, and the Palestinian people as a net loser, within the Palestinian community there are also winners and losers. The current leadership of the PLO seems to have gained ascendancy, what with lucrative contracts, political appointments, and authority over the new Palestinian police force as its prize. Relative to Israeli power, this of course is almost laughable, but relative to the refugees in Lebanon, Syria and Jordan as well as the poor and landless in Gaza, it represents a considerable amount. What makes it particularly disquieting for the majority of Palestinians is that no system of accountability has yet been instituted. A great leader sitting in Tunis (or perhaps later in Jericho) can appoint a US bank and a team of Moroccan and Israeli financial advisers to be his 'experts' for handling internationally donated funds to 'the Palestinian people', and as yet no-one can ask why this has been done, and by what authority and in whose interest such people are allowed to determine the future course of Palestinian national development. The new draft constitution of the Palestinian entity says nothing about ceding authority to the people, but is quite specific about handing everything to the President (or however he proposes to describe himself) so that he may unilaterally determine what either gets done or does not get done inside Gaza and Jericho. Is this state of affairs and are these Palestinian winners what the immense struggle of the people has been about? Has the goal of the national effort to regain Palestinian rights only been to grant the current Palestinian leadership in Tunis the mantle of unrestricted authority over a tiny fraction of their homeland?

The great German critic and philosopher Walter Benjamin once wrote that 'whoever emerged victorious participates to this day in the triumphal procession in which the present rulers step over those who are lying prostrate'. It is the duty of the historian therefore to provide a reminder of that fact, in which the losers who are lying prostrate and forgotten are connected to the victors that strut and parade over their bodies before the world. In the Palestinian case, there can be no better way of doing this than to recount the experiences of a remarkable individual – Hanna Mikhail (Abu Omar) – who gave his life in 1976 in order that the principles and goals of 'the Palestinian revolution' (as it was then called) could be safeguarded and realized. When I think of the present state of affairs, with so much that has been discarded and voluntarily abandoned in our history, when the doctrines of realism and pragmatism are trumpeted by smug and shameless winners, and when a shabby, undemocratic Palestinian protectorate under Israeli rule is proclaimed as the fulfilment of our aspirations, I am also led inevitably to think of Hanna Mikhail, and in particular his dedication and principled course of action on behalf of his people.

I first met him in the late 1950s in the United States. I was a student at Princeton at the time, he a student (exactly my age) at Haverford College, a distinguished Quaker university about fifty miles from Princeton. He came to Haverford from Ramallah, where he had graduated from the Friends School; I from an American boarding school and before that from Victoria College in Egypt. He was studying chemistry, I literature. I was immediately struck both by his extraordinary personal modesty and civility, and by his very sharp intellect. In those days, neither of us was political: Ramallah was part of Jordan, and the Arab world at the time was dominated by Gamal Abdul Nasser, whose message of Arab nationalism included but did not stress the special nature of the Palestinian struggle to regain the rights of its dispossessed and dispersed native Arab inhabitants. Both these contexts in a sense were not really ours. After getting our BAs, we both ended up as graduate students at Harvard. I recall seeing him there during the 1960s, and I also recall him telling me that he had changed from chemistry to Middle East Studies (he became a student of H. A. R. Gibb, the famous British Orientalist who had just moved from Oxford to Harvard). I myself had very little to do with the Middle East field – my concentration was on English and comparative literature – but I do remember that Hanna described his switch as a necessary one for someone like himself who needed to know more about the historical traditions and culture of his people.

In 1965 or 1966, I saw him in New York; he was teaching Arabic at Princeton and had just divorced his American wife. Our meetings then were infrequent, since I lived in New York whereas he was only an occasional visitor. After 1967 we lost touch, even though I knew from a common friend that Hanna had moved to the University of Washington in Seattle to become an assistant professor of Middle East Studies there. I did not see him again until the summer of 1970. Like every Arab of my generation, I had been deeply affected and indeed traumatized by the 1967 War, and subsequently stirred into political engagement by the emergence of the Palestinian Resistance movement, as it was then known. In August 1970, I travelled to Jordan to see for myself what 'our' movement had become. Kamal Nasir was a distant relative and good friend, and it was he who put me in touch with various comrades in the movement when I got to Amman. Among them of course was Hanna (the two men were both from Ramallah); I was unprepared for the transformation in my gentle, even pacifist old friend, who had now become a full-time partisan, a member of Fateh and a superbly effective information officer in charge of journalists and other outside visitors.

The main thing that struck me at the outset was the grandeur and generosity of his gesture in coming to Amman in the first place. He was a Harvard Ph.D. with a secure academic job in the United States. His future as a scholar and professor was assured. Instead, he gave all that up for the uncertainties, not to say the dangers of a volunteer's position in a popular movement that had barely begun, was about as insecure as it was possible to be in a volatile and hostile Arab environment, and above all had proposed for itself the all-but-insane goal of the liberation of Palestine. I never detected any uncertainty on his part about his decision to return. He never alluded to what he had left behind, and he always communicated to me the solid commitment of a man who had set the course of his life according to the magnificent principles of emancipation and enlightenment for his people from which he was never to budge. From then on he remained a Fateh militant, yet I never heard him utter a silly cliché or the slightest pomposity. In time, he acquired considerable authority and prestige within the movement; but, unlike many of his counterparts, he did not abuse or bully underlings with his superior rank and attainments.

Like Kamal Nasir, Hanna Mikhail came from a Christian background; this is something I share with both. As I think about it, the three of us in fact had very different educations and we came to the Palestinian struggle from extremely divergent perspectives. Kamal was a Baʿathist originally; Hanna was a Quaker graduate and a Middle Eastern scholar; I was almost completely Western in my education and knowledge. None of us however felt that we were members of a minority, although of course we were. Each of us in his own way regarded our heritage as Arab Islamic and our cultural perspectives as internationalist. Palestine was a liberation ideal, not a provincial movement for municipal self-rule under foreign tutelage. We saw it as an integral unit within the liberation movements of the Third World – secular, democratic, revolutionary.

Hanna, for example, was a scholar of Arab Islamic thought; that to him furnished a traditional continuity for later generations of Arabs to forge anew in their own efforts for national revival and freedom. On the other hand, none of us denied or felt anything but pride in the family and communal background that may have made us seem different to many of our fellow-Palestinians. But, for the three of us, the Christian communities from which we emerged were elements in the larger mosaic of Arab, Islamic and Third World anti-colonial movements, of which we were proud to be a part, different perhaps but never separate. Both Hanna and Kamal always impressed me, a relatively pedestrian Arabic-speaker and writer, with the eloquence and clarity of their language, which I have always since striven to emulate.

Hanna and I stood next to each other at a mass rally in Amman just before Black September. Yasser Arafat was declaiming from the balcony of a small house that 'we' had turned down the Rogers Plan and that the 15,000 Iraqi troops in Jordan had just committed themselves to 'us'. Hanna took me to meet Arafat just after the speech, but there were too many people around to say very much except the routine greetings that such occasions usually afford. But I distinctly remember Hanna's discomfort around Arafat. Both of us, I think, felt the power of the man's melodramatic oratory, but we also sensed that, though he could speak the language of liberation, he was a great actor and a supreme political animal with only a tenuous relationship to the truth. The Iraqi troops were not helpful, of course.

In 1972–3, I spent my academic sabbatical year in Beirut where I saw quite a lot of Hanna, whom I had begun to know as Abu Omar, in charge of student contacts, journalists and various segments of the by now growing Palestinian presence in Lebanon. I never knew or visited him where he lived, nor until later did I know much about his personal life. During those years before his death in 1976, he seemed to me to have immersed himself completely in his role as a political officer in the movement. In dress, manner and style of life, he struck me as ascetic in the extreme. He put on a little weight, but I never saw him wear anything but khaki fatigues, he never drove a car, and in his manner he never affected anything but a simple, austere rhetoric. He was always anxious to listen. Alone among my Palestinian comrades, when he asked me a question about developments in the United States he would actually wait for me to answer; usually when I would be asked the same question by some of the other intellectuals and Abus, I would be the one who would have to listen to a ninety-minute lecture on what was happening in America, most of it gleaned from *Time* magazine and the Beirut rumour exchange. I remember talking with Hanna about the anti-Vietnam war movement, about Noam Chomsky and others whose work he respected, and about developments in the military-industrial complex. I think by that time he had become a Marxist, but how different from his colleagues in the progressive movement he was! His vocabulary was full of observations about the human sufferings of people, of deprivation and nobility, of tragedy and hope, of powerlessness and optimism.

Two episodes in Beirut have remained especially clear in my memory. Hanna would often visit me in the little room I used in my house as a study. As we sat going over the latest Israeli raid on Nabatiye, their American planes raining down terror and punishment on innocent Palestinian and Lebanese civilians, I was so upset at the viciousness of our enemies that I asked him: 'Do you feel any hatred for them?' Never was I so flabbergasted when first he expressed surprise at my question, and second when he said: 'No, I don't think I can'. I saw in a flash both his essential gentleness as a human being and how much more sophisticated politically than me he was: he had affiliated himself with a movement that protected him from transient and ultimately not very useful emotions, so that a long-term political philosophy and commitment might develop instead. Hanna's answer taught me a lot about dedication and patience.

The second episode took place in early October 1972. I was at home with my family when, late at night, the phone rang. It was Hanna asking whether he could bring Jean Genet round to see me. At first I thought he was joking, since for me Genet was a giant of contemporary literature, and a visit from him was about as probable as one from Proust or Thomas Mann. No, Hanna said, I'm really serious; could we come now? They appeared fifteen minutes later and stayed for several hours. I have written elsewhere about what Genet said and did during that time, but Hanna's role needs some comment here. It is clear from *Le Captif amoureux* – Genet's posthumously published book on his love for the Palestinians – that Abu Omar was a crucial figure for him as guide, friend, trusted confidant. Hanna's French wasn't extraordinarily good, but he could manage. As Genet and I talked that night, Hanna sat quietly in the shadows, making an occasional interjection, answering a question, laughing at one of Genet's frequent *aperçus*. He never forced himself into the discussion, but instead remained as a patient, modest and enabling presence. Genet seems to have felt that, like many of the Palestinians to whom he grew close, Hanna represented a kind of purity and even personal, unselfish carelessness about himself that to the great French writer contained the essence of the

Palestinian revolution, its wonderful gaiety, its awesome internal power, its beautiful ideals. And I felt exactly those things about Hanna as he sat there with Genet. He told me later that he admired Genet because of his special poetical insight into 'our' doings, and that, he felt, was much more enriching than dry, textbook political analysis. By sitting there as he did – even though, without Hanna, Genet and I would not have met – Abu Omar embodied the prevailingly generous and unconventional principles of the Palestinian revolution. It was a moment of illumination for me.

After the Lebanese Civil War began, I saw Hanna in Beirut only intermittently, but we always kept in close touch. As the head of the Quaker community in Lebanon, my father-in-law Emile Cortas presided over the simple wedding ceremony that joined Hanna and Jehan Helou in a Quaker marriage ceremony (required by Lebanese law), and that fact brought us together for a few social occasions. It was also then that I grasped how Hanna had slowly begun to gather around himself a group of like-minded Fateh members (Fateh for him was the only movement to which he could belong because, he once told me, it was broad enough to represent all the people) who were dissatisfied with the political direction taken by the reigning powers. Hanna was against the abuse of power, he was against ostentatious spending and garish lifestyles, and he was one of the first to lament the appalling influence of petro-dollars. He soon refused to have anything to do with foreign journalists and dignitaries, believing his task to be 'our' self-education. He retained the deliberate, attractive and self-effacing manner of the truly gifted teacher. He neither preached nor scolded. Yet he unfailingly expressed his conviction in the principles of popular struggle and revolutionary transformation that were crucial to any real Palestinian victory. Once I recall that he lamented to me the folly of Palestinian involvement in Lebanese affairs; he was prophetic, since this was to lead to the disasters of 1982. But he also distrusted conventional Arab politics, a trivial copy of which Palestinian politics had become. Above all, he scorned the cult of the gun and of the personality: these he knew supplied superficial and immediate satisfaction, but they were too easily exploited by the opportunistic and unprincipled.

In the months before his death, I was impressed with how his dissenting ideas had spread within Fateh in Beirut. He told me of a trip he took to North Vietnam and of how that had strengthened his conviction in selfless dedication and careful organisation and discipline. I had also begun to surmise – I have no hard information on which to rely, except the somewhat precarious evidence I deduced from friends of his – that he had begun to trouble the leadership with his earnest dissent and the growing influence that he exerted on those who worked with him. I must say in all honesty and sadness that his untoward disappearance and subsequent death in 1976 seemed to me not to have been so inconvenient for those in Fateh who found his opposition to political manoeuvring, cronyism and the bending of principle so irritatingly well-represented by Hanna's practice and theory. His disappearance while on what appeared to be a foolishly contrived mission to go by a small and unprotected boat from Beirut to Tripoli in waters that were constantly patrolled by Israeli and Phalanges forces seemed like the result of incredibly poor planning and a great deal of unacceptable carelessness. For years after this tragic cadence to his life, I often thought that that ill-fated voyage had robbed the Palestinian movement of one of its most principled and humanely inspired cadres. No wonder then that so many of his friends and especially his brave widow Jehan refused to accept the fact of his capture as final, and no wonder that so many of us had a strong stake in keeping hope alive for his release and return.

It seems to me, however, that his tragically foreshortened life has acquired an even more considerable significance today. Hanna Mikhail is not among the victors in the march of today's peace process. His compatriots are still under military occupation. His co-workers in Lebanon and elsewhere are still in exile. Worst of all, in my opinion, the ideas and principles for which he quite literally lived and died, principles of humane liberation, decent coexistence between Arabs and Jews, social and economic justice for men and women, all these have been put in temporary eclipse not just by the cynicism of the Israeli Labour party, but also by his own equally cynical movement. A new ascendancy stressing pragmatic realism now advocates unconditional friendship with a United States that still donates $5 billion per year to Israel, and that still opposes Palestinian self-determination as that phrase is understood everywhere else in the world.

More perniciously, this ascendancy believes that deals between highflying financiers are better for 'the people' than that people's own efforts. Hanna Mikhail's whole life was focused on a searching radicalism, unsatisfied with the vulgar clichés of politics as business, unconvinced by empty slogans of triumphalist demagoguery, scornful of lazy incompetence and favouritism. Hanna stood for principles and ideals, not as airy abstractions, but as concrete manifestations in everyday life, among ordinary men and women, for Arab and Jew alike. In recalling Hanna Mikhail as a friend and as a historical figure in the struggle for human freedom and knowledge, we need to accept what Walter Benjamin suggests is the historian's task which, he says, is to dissociate oneself from the so-called march of progress, then to provide a different history *against* the main, apparently victorious current.

Hanna Mikhail was a true intellectual. What I have said about him neither sentimentalizes nor exaggerates his qualities. He retained his original Quaker modesty and plainness. But, as an intellectual should, he lived according to his ideas and never tailored his democratic, secular values to suit new masters and occasions. For all Palestinians today, and in stark contrast to the great sell-out and abject surrender of our leaders, he represents a distinguished role model, a man who did not debase himself or his people. Why? Because he *lived* his ideas, and died for them. It is as simple as that. By his example, Hanna Mikhail admonishes those who have outlived him for a while.

Foreword

BIANCAMARIA SCARCIA AMORETTI

For me, Hanna Mikhail was and remains Abu Omar. Wa'il Zuaiter introduced me to him in Rome in, I think, 1969, probably on his way back from attending an important student demonstration in Milan. I did not know that he was an Orientalist, whose professional field was Islam and specifically medieval Islam, until a couple of years ago when his wife, Jehan Helou, sent me the text of his thesis to read with a view to possible publication. I understand that Abu Omar did not want to publish it without developing it and making some amendments which were, however, not to see the light owing to the tragic sudden end to his life.

I met him because I had begun to be involved in Palestine and I considered him simply a representative of the Palestinian resistance. I had followed the same path as many intellectuals of my generation had done: a left-wing militant and Third Worlder in the name of Algeria and Vietnam. I first approached the Palestinian Question after the Six Days' War, on the one hand because of the blatantly unbalanced reaction of public opinion in favour of the aggressor, considered the victim, and on the other by my own desire, after obtaining tenure in 1968, to give my University teaching a content which went beyond traditional programmes and which bore witness, as far as possible, to a true commitment towards the realities we were studying.

Our meeting was a felicitous one in the sense that a form of syntony grew up between us. Knowing today that we followed the same profession, I am tempted to attribute this to a common cultural matrix, a shared store of knowledge concerning the Arab world and Islam which reduced the gap between someone like him, who belonged to that world even though he had not been born into the Muslim faith, and someone like me, who necessarily looked at that world from the outside even if very sympathetically.

But my memories, which are not very specific (for we all agreed that Ho Chi Minh was right when he said that history has to be made and not told), give pride of place to the political aspects, including a meeting at my house with the well-known French orientalist Maxime Rodinson, whom Abu Omar had expressed the wish to see. The only unpolitical detail I remember about that day is that he appreciated a Sicilian orange and fennel salad almost as if it were an exotic dish. We did things together and held and attended meetings.

My role was that of escort and interpreter, though in fact his human and political charisma was such that I grew far more involved than I had originally expected. If I had to attribute the merit of my introduction to the history of Palestine and the world of the Palestinian resistance to anyone, after Wa'il Zuaiter my thoughts would turn to Abu Omar. Looking back on what we did, I seem to remember that we visited local branches of the Communist Party, attended trade-union meetings and held meetings with my students (for one of which they prepared a 'sit-in'). Films were shown and abundant documentation presented, the personal theories of the organizers were expressed and everything discussed with the people directly involved, namely the Palestinians represented by Abu Omar. This was probably in 1970 or 1971. At the time, the student movement followed two trends. These were distinguished by two slogans 'Red Palestine' and 'Free Palestine', but there was no reason then for the existence of divisions and contrasts inside the Palestinian resistance, and, because of that, for years, though this group of students held to their ideas of what the future of Palestine ought to be, they worked together to the best of their ability.

Though I cannot give exact dates for our meetings, I know that I never saw him again after Wa'il Zuaiter's assassination in 1972.

Neither Abu Omar nor I was in the habit of attributing importance to the bureaucratic or hierarchical role held by anyone working within the Organization. I only knew later that he had become a member of 'Tribunale Russell II', which came to be based in Italy, when Lelio Basso, the president, mentioned it after I became one of his regular collaborators.

I learnt indirectly, mainly from Jehan, about the events in his life. And personally I am left with the enrichment of having met him and collaborated with him, and the many-faceted regret that I did not do more, that I did not get to know him more in depth, that I cannot hear his voice explaining what is happening now, in order to be able to overcome doubts, hesitations and – why not – disappointments.

About twenty years ago, D. P. Little, in an article[1] on the studies and research on Māwardī, expressed the hope that Hanna Mikahil's doctorate thesis[2] would be published. He maintained that this thesis deserved 'wider circulation'[3] not only because it contained new elements, such as the definition of Māwardī as a 'free thinker'[4] and, consequently, an exponent of neither Ashʿarism nor the muʿtazila, but also because it was a work which, unlike 'almost all the studies of Māwardī – limited to one of his books, *al-Aḥkām al-sulṭāniyya*, or to a part of it'[5] – considered the author's entire production and presented a kind of analysis 'from the inside' based on a comparison of Māwardī's ideas as illustrated in his various texts.

This hope and this evaluation are still fundamentally valid since even H. Laoust's imposing work, which came out almost at the same time as Mikhail discussed his thesis[6] (and which I will frequently be quoting), does not fill the lacunae mentioned by Little. I therefore consider it important that *Politics and Revelation: Māwardī and After* should finally see the light: a postumous homage to Mikhail and a precious contribution to present-day Islamic studies.

This in itself is enough to explain the reasons for the publication of Mikhail's work, for in fact there is little to add to his reconstruction of 'Māwardī's thought'. As far as I know, there are no new editions[7] of texts by Māwardī which would make a new general survey of his political theory necessary. On the contrary, the works which have made an in-depth study of any specific aspect from 1968 to the present day (for example, N. Calder's article[8] on the Friday prayer and the juridical theory of 'government' confirm Mikhail's conclusions, particularly where two aspects of Māwardī's thought are concerned. These are the legitimation of innovative administrative practices through their insertion into the context of the *sharīʿa*, and the pre-eminence of the Caliphal institution over other governmental instances, which he stresses a number of times in spite of his awareness, which Calder too refers to,[9] that by then the Caliphate was a kind of 'constitutional monarchy' which claimed a theoretical primacy insofar as it was theoretical source of authority which, however, was devoid of effective power.

The theme under discussion is that of the nomination of the imām, who must direct the Friday prayer which, as we know, is particularly important both on a religious plane – it is the communal prayer – and a political plane – it is the seat in which the Caliph, the recognized authority in office, is mentioned. Māwardī held that the right to make this nomination rests with the Caliph or one of his delegates who is the effective holder of power. Further comparison with a contemporary of Māwardī, Sharīf al-Murtaḍā (an exponent of Imamite Shīʿism who died in 436/1044), supports this opinion concerning Māwardī's innovative attempt to absorb the political institutions of the time, as they were organized and administered by the court bureaucracy, into the sphere of the *fiqh*.[10] In fact, discussing this same theme of the Friday prayer,[11] Sharīf al-Murtaḍā carefully avoids making any statements concerning the problem of the imām's nomination and merely recognizes the Sultan's pre-eminence, namely his right to act as imām if he is present. He next formulates a hierarchy of those who may or may not carry out the functions of imām, without giving any particular significance to the office. In doing this, he falls in line with the positions of Sarakhsī and Shīrāzī[12] (analyzed in the above-mentioned article), which are not those of Māwardī, even though the Shīʿite author admits the possibility of enhancing the role of learned men and clerics, a role which is played down in Māwardī to the extent that it is nothing but the expression of power.[13]

However, one aspect of Māwardī has been quite consistently reconsidered, and that is the historical contextualization of his work. While Hanna Mikhail focuses his attention on the evolution of the political theories of the time and presents a rather complex picture of the political debate which was taking place among learned men, attempting, in this perspective, to exemplify the typology of the various currents, tendencies and schools with which Māwardī presents similarities or discordances, more recent criticism often gives pride of place to the analysis of Māwardī's political role and refers to this role as the interpretative key to his thought.

In this sense, Laoust's above-mentioned article,[14] which serves as reference and prototype,[15] is fundamental. Laoust starts with the statement that the *al-Aḥkām al-sulṭāniyya* is 'a treatise composed at the request of the authorities to defend the legitimacy of the ʿAbbāsid Caliphate and restore, as far as possible, its prestige and power'.[16] This leads to the hypothesis of the dating of the text, after 1039, and, in particular, the explanation of the reading of Māwardī's judgments concerning Islam's past history, namely the total absence of any form of criticism towards the 'orthodox' Caliphal dynasties, including the Omiyad dynasty which was ousted by the ʿAbbāsids, as the justification of Yazīd's action against al-Ḥusayn ibn ʿAlī at Karbalā' proves. The essential motivation remains the need to contain the eversive tendency represented by Ismāʿīlism, which triumphed in Cairo under the Fāṭimids, and to contest the power of the *wazīr*-Buyids, who were Shīʿites too, though harder to place since whether they belonged to Zaydism or Twelver Imāmism remains an open question. To this we must add the problematic relationship with the emerging power of the Seljuks which was to end (thanks also to Māwardī) in a basic acceptance of the Seljuk Sulṭanate as a bargaining instrument with the Buyids on the one hand and as an instrument of opposition against the Fāṭimids on the other.

The importance of Māwardī's diplomatic missions between 1032 and 1038 (for a reconstruction see Laoust's article[17]) rests in fact on the interdependence that the scholars cull between Māwardī's action, which confirmed among other things the impossibility of granting the Buyid Amīr's request for a title – *sulṭān al-aʿẓam*, or *malik al-umam* or *malik al-mulūk* – to which only the Caliph had a right (in spite of the fact that this refusal jeopardized the negotiations over the donations due to the Caliph himself) and the theory which Māwardī explains in the *al-Aḥkām*.[18]

Though Māwardī may have been a kind of ʿAbbāsid agent who operated in defence of the Caliphate during the historical moment of crisis which it was going through, it seems to me reductive to limit the matter to an interpretation of this kind. In fact, this would exclude or reduce the theoretical importance of Māwardī's work, which is valid as such regardless of the period and contingent situation in which it was written. As I have mentioned before, Hanna Mikhail has chosen to focus on the significance of this theory through a systematic comparison between what had already been developed before Māwardī and what, through his more or less direct influence, his successors accepted or refuted.

Besides, any interest in continuing to devote attention to his work stems precisely from its impact on Islamic political thought.

Māwardī is quoted in almost every summary of political thought in medieval Islam,[19] though opinions concerning him vary. Some people maintain that his thought has been overrated,[20] while others consider his works fundamental.[21]

But the matter is presented awkwardly in these terms, and Mikhail's work helps us again to reorganize the whole question. In fact, if we start from the picture he presents, where Māwardī is placed in a sequence which goes from Ibn al-Muqaffaʿ at least until Ibn Taymiyya, we see that it is possible to formulate a periodisation concerning the evolution of political theories between the end of the eighth century and the thirteenth century – a period which embraces the height of the ʿAbbāsid Caliphate, its decline and its definitive disappearance from the political scene.

Māwardī himself was aware of representing a stage along a course whose outcome he attempted to determine. Thus he says: 'I have summarized in this book [*Tashīl al-naẓar wa taʿjil al-ẓafar*] the precepts of government that have been masterfully laid down by the ancients', but he also maintains, in the same text, that 'Previous works are not an adequate substitute for a book that, in clarifying the requirements of divine Law and the well-known principles of government, conforms with religion and the world'.[22]

We will attempt to reconstruct this periodization. To begin with, if we exclude the political notions implicit in the various treatises concerning the *Kharāj*, the 'Mirrors for Princes' offer a cross-section of the image which the ʿAbbāsid power wished to mediate in function of the affirmation of an ideology which ought to guarantee a wide consensus, regardless of what the Caliphs actually did. This operation tended to systematize ideas that were still fluid concerning both the concept of authority and that of State. The formal rather than substantial dependence of this production on the Sassanian model[23] allowed both those who accomplished similar operations and those who commissioned them to maintain a kind of ambiguity which could be useful in the case of contestations concerning the emerging ideology. On the other hand, this can be verified through a comparison of the goals of the 'Mirrors for Princes' with the imposition of a historiography that was becoming official (Ṭabarī is the most significant example of this) and which was following the line of the powers in office.[24] This first phase was followed by a second one which Māwardī himself brought to its conclusion. The decentralization which was occurring in the empire, both where formal obedience to the Caliphate still held (as in the oriental Iranic provinces) and where there was antagonism to it (as in Shī'ī, and in particular Ismā'īlī, activism), did not yet seem an irreversible phenomenon; and the systematization accomplished in the preceding centuries, mainly the ninth and tenth, seemed to some extent to have been interiorized in the Muslim collective conscience. This involved, among other things, the assumption of the idea of unity – the unity of the authorities, the unity of the State, the unity of the community – as something which could not be renounced when defining a person's way of being. One has to come on the one hand to Ibn Taymiyya and on the other to Ibn Khaldūn for the plurality of power and State to be accepted not only as a given fact but as an element which did not question the unity of the community of believers (the only unity which continued to be both credible and possible in view of the fact that its existence depended on will and self-definition and not necessarily on an operative institution[25]).

The stage which came after Māwardī was emblematically represented by Niẓām al-Mulk,[26] whose incontestable interpretation of the connection between practice and theory was based entirely on historicity (this was also attributed, as we said before, to Māwardī). Niẓām al-Mulk acted as counterpoint (or vice versa, if the reader prefers) to al-Ghazālī, who ended the work of systematization. The result of this was that the evolution of political theory – and Ibn Taymiyya and Ibn Khaldūn adequately prove this – ran side by side with the reassertion of the validity of Ghazalian systematization. It was as if the concept of 'orthodoxy', which had been relatively fluid until al-Ghazālī, coagulated into an orthodox 'system' of thought whose rigidifying effects began to be denounced. An author like Badie,[27] for example, bases his analysis of the medieval sources of Islamic political thought on three authors: Māwardī, whom he recognizes as an innovator[28] for having attributed to the Caliph the authority to delegate power to his representatives while at the same time placing the Caliphal institution within revelation; Ibn Taymiyya who, according to him, confirms the passage from state of legitimacy to state of necessity mentioned above; and al-Ghazālī who, in the name of the basic need of maintaining social order, not only theorizes renouncing the right to resist a possibly unjust or inadequate power but also moves the reflection on power from its divine origin to its destination, which can be summed up as follows: 'In order to be legitimate, power must in the first place exist; men must obey; Princes and Caliphs must respect God's law under the supervision of the learned men (*ʿulamā'*)', thus providing both theoretical and political motivation for the 'quietism' which distinguished the political debate of the following centuries.[29]

Both Māwardī's innovative significance and the plausibility of the above-mentioned periodization can be verified in another way, by comparing them with the political literature of a movement like that of Imāmite Shīʿa which, since it did not present the risks which Ismāʿīlism presented for the Caliphate, 'politically suited' the Buyids who were the effective holders of power in Baghdad after 945.[30] This comparison is not an original one,[31] but it must be seen in a perspective which does not simply describe the ideological cultural atmosphere of the period.

Hanna Mikhail, quoting an authority like Kulaynī, says that by Māwardī's time the Twelver Shīʿites had moved from politics to ethics, having ascertained that their rise to power was unlikely.[32] This is exact if we see an acceptance of official power and the relative deferment of the perfect kingdom to the advent of the Mahdī as a call to obedience in the given situation.

This statement does not hold if, on the other hand, we consider the ambit of political production (even if exclusively theoretical) of Imāmism. A text like Shaykh al-Mufid's *Kitāb al-Irshād*, a compendium of the lives of the Imāms composed around 990,[33] can be interpreted politically if we analyse the part devoted to ʿAlī as an indirect formulation of the meaning of Imāmate and of the characteristics which the person chosen to represent him must guarantee. The theory of the *afḍal*, the best of men, as the only person destined to the Imāmate is obviously taken up, but it must be considered as a premise to what al-Mufīd himself says concerning the *qiyām* of the hidden Imām, which, even if in eschatological terms, sums up the idea of good government under the dual aspect of the governor and the governed.[34]

Sharīf al-Murtaḍā, in the same text which we used for our considerations on the Friday prayer,[35] opens his chapter on the Imāmate with the need for its existence in 'every epoch in order to bring people closer to good and draw them away from evil', and only after this, and after enumerating the Imām's qualities (his being *afḍal* and *maʿṣūm*), he presents himself as a Shīʿite, in the sense that he attributed purely theoretical value to his statement at the time of writing.

On the other hand, we can take the comparison up again when al-Murtaḍā defines the *ʿadl* which should distinguish the Imām. All this leads to the conclusion that the Shīʿite political thought of Māwardī's time, like his own thought, lay halfway between a realistic stand in the face of the real situation and a reassertion of the basic principles of the theory underlying the professed credo, with the prospect of legitimizing the action which can be foreseen in view of the circumstances without renouncing the hypothesis of a possibly different outcome in an undefined future. It is as if we were saying that Māwardī's course concerning the elements which scholars consider innovative ran parallel to or even preceded that of Imāmite Shīʿa, which necessarily had to update its political theory. Of course, where Shīʿism is concerned, these were only allusions, suggestions rather than statements, but they allow us to establish the close of a phase in the development of political thought and the opening of the next one, which was to find its most complete expression in the mid-thirteenth century. In fact, when we read Naṣīr al-dīn al-Ṭūsī's *Risālat al-Imāma*,[36] which is a real treatise of political theory, we see how great the difference is. On the one hand we have a real datum – the fact that the Shīʿites did not seize power – which is so taken for granted that it is not mentioned even indirectly through stressing the symbolic value of the *ghayba* and the expectation of the *qiyām*, both themes which are dealt with hurriedly in sentences such as 'This is not an absurd consideration for those who consider the Most High God powerful and wise'.[37] On the other hand, the treatise is based on logic and its author seems to be content with the recognition of a formal coherence which does not primarily need to be translated into an operative political plane, nor is this required of it.

All that we have said so far illustrates how indebted studies on medieval Islam are to the present work. But there is an ulterior, political, reason for its publication: the present Islamic revival seeks its referents in specific medieval characters, one of whom is certainly Ibn Taymiyya. An author who is both objective and involved[38] tells us that Ibn Taymiyya's work 'constitutes an effort of reflection, for which there is almost no equivalent, to approach the problems of Islam right after the fall of Baghdad through the ideal developed by the ancestors of the *Ahl al-sunna wa'l-jamaʿa* who laid the foundations of the Sunnite political-juridical-religious system'. He also tells us that the merit of having ensured 'the unity of the *umma*, its defence through writing against heresies and through the *jihād* against external aggressions' goes to Ibn Taymiyya.

Now if it is true that the history of medieval Muslim political thought presents a continuous line marked by changes and adjustments but not by breaks and lacunae, some reference to Māwardī (another theorist in a class with Ibn Taymiyya[39] and in fact his predecessor) is justified in the perspective of a clarification of the matrices of specific positions in so-called present-day radical and militant Islam.

In fact, though Hanna Mikhail discussed his thesis in 1968 and nothing at the time pointed towards any of the successive developments in Islamic territory, we cannot exclude the possibility that the motivations for his choice of subject did not embrace the prophetic one of verifying whether the past offered material for a possible renewal of Islamic vitality and whether a logical (i.e. not fundamentalist and not confessional) sequence, which would allow for a search for roots not in contrast with modernity and everything connected with it on the political plane, could be traced back to this material.

On the other hand, Mikhail must have borne in mind the debate[40] which started in colonial times and continued during the first national experiments, especially in the Arab world, concerning the denunciation of 'unjust' sovereigns and the revival of the concepts which would legitimate rebellion against them. The need for a sovereign, which only in some cases was postulated as a return to the Caliphate,[41] was asserted starting from the negation of the right of an unworthy sovereign to claim obedience. A similar attitude is widespread today too.

The Iranian revolution was more *against* someone (the Shāh) than *for* someone (the *faqih*). The ambiguity concerning what Islamic government means – an ambiguity which emerges emblematically in the fact that, using almost the same arguments, some people maintain that the form of government most congruous with the authentic spirit of Islam is a republican government and others, on the contrary, favour a monarchical ideal[42] – is overcome in the fundamental homogeneity of the definitions of the 'enemy', the West, and above all everything which resembles and imitates it. Undoubtedly this confirms or ratifies the Islamic political ideal, at least in general terms. The responsibility for the fact that this ideal has not been explicitly actualized is attributed to the absence of a 'just sovereign'. This is exemplified in ʿAbd al-Salām Faraj's *al-Fārida al-ghā'iba*, when he says: 'The laws which govern Muslims today are impious laws ... since the Caliphate was definitely abolished, in 1924, all the laws of Islam have been uprooted and replaced with laws imposed by the impious ...'.[43] However, there are no echos of Māwardī's theory concerning the Caliphate in present-day Islamic thought, though it is interesting to note how an ideologist like al-Mawdūdī transfers the characteristics required of a Caliph to the *Majlis- i Shūrā*, the highest institution in the state he preconizes, and only after this to the head of the state.[44]

And Sayyid Quṭb himself takes up an analogous position when he says that Atatürk should not have abolished the Caliphate, in spite of the fact that the Caliph-Imām is only a deputy (*nā'ib*) of the community for the execution of divine Law and has no other rights or powers.[45]

In contemporary Muslim political thought, the political subject par excellence is the community in a relationship of interdependence with the 'leader', according to the dictate of Ibn Khaldūn.[46] But the community must perform the functions which medieval Islam, and in particular Māwardī, considered the task of the sovereign. Two elements which Māwardī considered significant in the definition of a political subject are equally so in present-day Islamic ideology. One of these is the positivity of the *jihād*, 'against those who obstinately refuse Islam after they have been invited to adhere to it, until they profess it or enter into the state of protection (*dhimma*)[47]' (according to Māwardī); 'offensive war ... destined to overthrow the existing political institutions or at least force those in charge to pay the *jizya*, to declare their capitulation ...; a dynamic, effective, active solicitation for the abolition of the laws and powers and ... the practical realization of the message of Islam in the form of a regime which ensures the government of men according to the *sharīʿa* ...' (according to someone like Sayyid Quṭb).[48] The other is the *ʿadl*, justice – a main theme in Mikhail's work – which, according to Māwardī, is an indispensable attribute both for the Caliph's electors (*ahl al-ikhtiyār*) and for possible aspirants to the office (*ahl al-imāma*),[49] as well as being the point of departure and ultimate goal of Islam in its political and social dimension for present-day Muslims.[50] The reference to justice as the informative criterion of human action needs no comment if it were not for a datum which we would like to stress as our conclusion.

Māwardī says that the Caliph's first duty is to uphold religion according to its principles, as defined by the consensus of the ancients.[51] Now the first possibility of putting the *ʿadāla* into practice lies in the execution of this obligation, which is like saying that Māwardī answered the needs of his historical moment, which was that of the Ismāʿīlī danger. However, this indication, taken in the context of theories on power and not in the context of its immediate historical implication, takes on the dimension of a cliché which the Muslim collective conscience can interiorize and turn to as a reference whenever it feels in danger, as it does today.

In this way, intolerance, which can even reach the point of formulating the need for the *jihād* within the *umma*, more or less consciously discovers a precedent. Deviations must be fought in the name of the ideal which is structured in political and social terms around the concept of justice. Of course it is the Koran and not the learned men of the past who are invoked, but the safeguarding of the community remains the goal to pursue: 'If only this *umma* had continued to consult its Qur'ān, ... to set up its rules and its laws ... its enemies would never have been able to strike it'.[52]

NOTES

1. D. P. Little, 'A new look to the *al-Aḥkām al-sulṭāniyya*', *Muslim World* 64 (1974), pp. 1–18.
2. *Māwardī: A Study in Islamic Political Thought*, a thesis presented by J. H. Mikhail, Harvard University, Cambridge MA, April 1968.
3. D. P. Little, op. cit., p. 6.
4. Ibid.
5. Ibid.
6. H. Laoust, 'La pensée et l'action politique de al-Māwardī (364–450/974–1058)', *Revue d'Etudes Islamiques* XXXVI (1968), pp. 11–12.
7. This is why we have not considered it necessary to update Mikhail's Bibliography. On the one hand, as he himself says, it is the one he used in the course of his work and therefore the footnotes refer to it; on the other, one of the purposes of this introduction is to acknowledge how little new material has come out on the subject during the last thirty years. It must be noted however that the subject has been taken in its more limited sense, i.e. concerning Māwardī himself, and not, as would also have been plausible, political theory in Islam. However the *al-Aḥkām al-sulṭāniyya* were republished in 1966 and again in Paris (Le Sycomore) in 1982 and the first volume of the *Adab al-qāḍī*, edited by Muḥyī Halāl Sarhān, came out in Baghdad in 1971. Finally, a new edition of the *Kitāb adab al-dunyā wa'l-dīn* with a commentary by Muḥammad Karīm Rajīh was published in Beirut in 1985.
8. N. Calder, 'Friday Prayer and the juristic theory of government: Sarakhsī, Shīrāzī, Māwardī', *Bulletin of the School of Oriental and African Studies* XLIX, 1 (1986), pp. 35–47.
9. Ibid., p. 47.
10. Ibid., p. 44.
11. Al-Sharīf ʿAlī ibn al-Ḥusayn al-Murtadā, *Juml al-ʿilm wa'l-ʿamal*, edited by Rashīd al-Ṣaffār, Najaf, 1968, pp. 74–6.
12. This is a kind of formal adherence to established authority and above all to the *ʿulamā'*, in the absence of the Imām in *ghayba*: cf. W. Madelung, 'Authority in Twelver Shiism in the Absence of the Imam', in *Religious Schools and Sects in Medieval Islam*, ch. X, Variorum Reprint, London, 1985, pp. 163–73, and particularly p. 166.
13. Calder, op. cit., p. 47.
14. See note 6.
15. See, for example, R. P. Mottahedeh, *Loyalty and Leadership in an Early Islamic Society*, Princeton University Press, 1980, p. 188; Mustapha Hogga, *Orthodoxie, Subversion et Réforme en Islam, Gazali et les Seljuqides*, Paris, 1993, pp. 34–5.

16. H. Laoust, op. cit., pp. 30–1.
17. Ibid., p. 77ff.
18. As Laoust points out, one can deduce, for example, the date of composition of the text from the result of these diplomatic missions.
19. See T. Nagel, *Staat und Glaubengemeinschaft im Islam*, Zurich and Munich, 1981; or E. I. J. Rosenthal, 'The role of the state in Islam: theory and the medieval practice', *Der Islam*, 1973, pp. 1–28; W. Kawtharānī, *al-Faqīh wa 'l-sulṭān*, Beirut, 1990, pp. 22–7.
20. For example, D. P. Little, op. cit., when (pp. 7–8) he analyzes the relationship between the works of Māwardī and those of Ibn al-Farrā'.
21. H. Laoust, in his *Les Schismes dans l'Islam*, Paris, 1983, p. 270, says that the *al-Aḥkām al-sulṭāniyya* are among the most important treatises on public law which have come down to us from Sunnism, together with Ibn Taymiyya's *Siyāsa shar'iyya*.
22. See above.
23. See B. Scarcia Amoretti, 'A proposito dell'ideologia mercantile negli *Specchi per Principi* nell'Islam medievale', in *Mercati e mercanti nell'alto Medioevo: l'area euroasiatica e l'area mediterranea*, Spoleto, 1993, pp. 799–826.
24. Idem, 'Islamic studies between acculturation and tradition: some remarks', in *The East and the Meaning of History*, Rome, 1994 (forthcoming).
25. See, both in support of the hypothesis of periodization proposed here and more generally on the subject of the community, A. K. S. Lambton, *State and Government in Medieval Islam*, Oxford University Press, 1981, pp. 83–102, devoted in particular to Māwardī.
26. The reference is obviously to his *Siyāsat-nāma*.
27. B. Badie, *Les deux Etats*, Paris, 1986 (quoted here from the Italian translation, Genoa, 1990, pp. 42–6).
28. See also A. al-Baghdadi, 'al-Māwardī's contribution to Islamic political thought', *Islamic Culture* 58 (1984), pp. 327–31.
29. To clarify the meaning of the terms, see B. Lewis, 'On the quietist and activist traditions in Islamic political writing', *Bulletin of the School of Oriental and African Studies* 49 (1986), pp. 141–7.
30. See Seyyed Hossein Nasr's 'Preface' to Shaykh al-Mufīd's *Kitāb al-Irshād*, London, 1981, p. xxi.
31. See, for example, H. Laoust, op. cit., p. 45ff.
32. See above.
33. See note 30. The translation is I. K. A. Howard's.
34. Ibid., in particular p. 541ff.
35. See note 11. This was not a specific choice. The text seemed to us indicative since it is a 'Summary' or index of the themes which have been considered in one way or another.
36. B. Scarcia Amoretti, '*La Risālat al-Imāma* di Naṣīr al-dīn Ṭūsī', *Rivista degli Studi Orientali* XLVII (1974). The translation is on pp. 249–63.
37. Ibid., particularly p. 262 and the commentary which follows, pp. 263–76.
38. We are referring here to Sadek Sallam, *Etre Musulman aujourd'hui*, Paris, 1989. We chose this author because he is not evidently in line with any specific movement or party.

39. Besides note 11, cf. the many works by Gibb and those by Rosenthal discussed and mentioned in the Bibliography, and E. Sivan, *Radical Islam, Medieval Theology and Modern Politics*, New Haven, CT, 1985.
40. See B. S. Amoretti, 'La concezione del "leader": religione e politica nell'Islam', *Rassegna di Teologia* XXVI (1985), pp. 514–28, particularly p. 523ff.
41. For example, Mahdism in Sudan on the one hand and the pro-Caliphate movement in India in the 1920s on the other.
42. The first case is exemplified by Khumaynī's *Wilāyat al-faqīh*, the second by Morocco (cf. F. Burgat, W. Douall, *The Islamic Movement in North Africa*, University of Texas, Austin, TX, 1993, p. 43).
43. See G. Kepel, *Le Prophète et le Pharaon*, Paris, 1984, p. 186ff.
44. See J. L. Esposito (ed.), *Voices of Resurgent Islam*, Oxford University Press, 1983, p. 124ff.
45. See O. Carré, *Mystique et Politique*, Paris, 1984, pp. 191–4.
46. The *Muqaddima*, translated by F. Rosenthal, New York, 1958, vol. 1, p. 385ff.
47. El-Mewerdi, *Le droit du Califat*, intro. and transl. by Comte L. Ostrorog, Paris, 1925, pp. 145–6.
48. See O. Carré, op. cit., p. 128.
49. M. Enger (ed.), *Maverdii Constitutiones politicae*, Bonn, 1853, p. 5 (Arabic num.).
50. For example, Sayyid Quṭb, *al-ʿAdāla al-ijtimaʿiyya fī'l-Islām*, 1949 (but published in Cairo in 1951).
51. See H. Laoust, op. cit., p. 55; but Ostrorog (p. 144) translates it as 'Accord de la Nation '.
52. Sayyid Quṭb, *Fī Ẓilāl al-Qur'ān*, 7th edn, Beirut, 1971, p. 679 (commentary to Qur'ān 5:12–13, concerning the fact that Moses did not enter the Promised Land), and D. Reiff Ashour, *L'esegesi coranica contemporanea (verses V, 20–16)*, unpublished thesis, University of Rome, academic year 1992-3.

Transliteration of Arabic Characters

The following conventions have been used throughout:

CONSONANTS

'	ء	ẓ	ظ
b	ب	'	ع
t	ت	gh	غ
th	ث	f	ف
j	ج	q	ق
ḥ	ح	k	ك
kh	خ	l	ل
d	د	m	م
dh	ذ	n	ن
r	ر	h	ه
z	ز	w	و
s	س	y	ي
sh	ش	ة	in pause: -a otherwise: -at
ṣ	ص		
ḍ	ض		
ṭ	ط		

VOWELS

Short vowels			*Long vowels*		*Doubled*	
					uww (final: ū)	وّ
fatḥa	a	َ	ā	ا ى	iyy (final: ī)	يّ
ḍamma	u	ُ	ū	و	*Diphthongs*	
					aw	وْ
kasra	i	ِ	ī	ي	ay	يْ

Introduction

This study in Islamic political thought attempts to examine two problems: the first, shared by all thought in Islam – indeed by all thought in any community that is the inheritor of a revealed message – is the relation of reason to revelation;[1] the second, a principal problem of political thought in particular, is the relation of politics to revelation.

A jurist-theologian was chosen as a focus of this book because for most Muslims the function of political thought is not to speculate normatively or to deduce empirically but to defend and elaborate God's revelation – two activities that, when systematically pursued, culminate in theology and jurisprudence respectively.[2] The choice of Māwardī (d. 1058) in particular was not so much for his effort to reconcile reason with revelation – an effort that received high praise from fellow Muslims[3] – as for his classic attempt to relate politics to revelation. Māwardī is to my knowledge the first Muslim to undertake a comprehensive deduction of the elements of Law that pertain to government. His formulation in the *Statutes of Government* is not only the first but also the most famous in Islamic history.[4]

Politics and Revelation rejects the crude determinism that sees ideas either as the determining force of history or as a mere superstructure of socioeconomic realities. Instead, the historical process is seen as a complex and continuous interaction between political ideals and realities. The book focuses on Sunnism, the historically prevalent form of Islam. But since it represents a variety of attitudes within broadly defined limits – limits that were defined by the rejection of specific opposing doctrines – Sunnism is not discussed in isolation.

This analysis is largely based on primary Muslim sources. It utilizes all of Māwardī's extant works, many of which are still in manuscript-form in various libraries of the world, and a large number of works (including some manuscripts) written between the eighth and nineteenth centuries.

As Islam achieved increasing importance as the ideological basis of empire, the defence of Muslim revelation became a political imperative. An attempt was made (by the Mu'tazila) to rationalize revelation. To this end, classical philosophy was consciously utilized. The revival of the philosophic tradition led to the growth of Muslim philosophy (Falsafa) which tended to subordinate or submerge revelation. The fear that revelation might threaten truths that are ultimately based on faith led to a fundamentalist reaction that either rejected the rationalization process altogether (Traditionalists – *ahl-ḥadīth*) or placed on it strict limitations (Ash'arites).

Māwardī's position in relation to the above intellectual currents has been the subject of controversy. He has been considered by some a Mu'tazilite and by others an Ash'arite. I show that he was neither. He was an independent thinker who rejected the Mu'tazilite position that the Qur'ān was uncreated but held firm to a rationalist theology which postulated the harmony of reason and revelation. Unlike his Ash'arite contemporaries, Māwardī viewed the spheres of reason and revelation as overlapping rather than mutually exclusive. In fact, being primarily a jurist, he was tolerant of various ways of defending the truth as long as agreement on the deduction of legal ordinances was assured.

While Māwardī's deduction of statutes of 'public' law was destined to occupy an important position in Islamic history, his rationalist theology did not fare so well. An anti-rationalist orientation eventually prevailed.

It is not surprising that, in a society where the individual was subordinate psychologically and socially to the authority of the group, individual reason should be subordinated to the authority of the revealed Book and Muḥammad's traditions. In addition to fundamentalism, the most important expression of Islam after the twelfth century was mysticism (Ṣūfism), which gave play not so much to individual reason as to emotional expression within strictly organized groups. Wherever theological activity survived (Ash'arism), it attempted to place strict limits on the rationalization process. Even Falsafa, the bastion of rationalism, gave way to theosophy which attempted to combine syllogistic proofs with 'intuitive' knowledge. Such an anti-rationalist orientation was not seriously challenged until the nineteenth century, when Muslim society was rudely awakened from its torpor by the impact of a modern 'rationalist' West.

Because Muḥammad was both Prophet and statesman and Islam served as the banner of an expanding empire, Muslims continued to claim that revelation as elaborated in the *sharī'a* (religious Law) should cover all aspects of life. This book shows how the *'ulamā'* (men of religion), having won the right to be sole guardians of the *sharī'a,* had to accept serious limitations as far as government was concerned. Māwardī, the first Muslim to attempt to spell out systematically the requirements of the *sharī'a* in regard to government, had to introduce a universal concept of justice as a supplementary criterion for evaluating governmental behaviour. Political justice as used by Muslim writers usually meant the provision of internal and external security, the protection of life and property, respect of custom, moderate taxation, and performance of limited public works especially in the river valleys where the maintenance of irrigation works was an important public function.

Given his neglect of the mechanics of government, Māwardī's attempt to incorporate the concept of political justice in the *sharī'a* was by no means successful. This failure of Māwardī, and of Islam in general, is dramatically illustrated by the fact that important religious works of later medieval times could state that a ruler might follow the *sharī'a* and still be unjust. Reactions to injustice ranged from absolute submission to revolution and tyrannicide. The response that eventually prevailed was quietism. Most of the *'ulamā'* fell in one of two groups: either they were satisfied to give the ruler a free hand in government as long as the *sharī'a* was respected and their role as its sole guardian was accepted, or, like Māwardī, they went further and insisted that the *'ulamā'* had the right to sit in judgment over the acts of the ruler to ensure that they were consonant with the requirements of religion and justice.

Needless to say, such a prescription could not check injustice, especially as rulers achieved greater control of the *'ulamā'* through increased institutionalization. The divergence between political ideals and realities reached crisis proportions in modern times not only because the ideal is now questioned but also because the expanded functions of government and its total claims make arbitrariness less tolerable.

As a by-product of this study, the scant biographical data on Māwardī was collected from sundry sources (Appendix B), the authorship and titles of Māwardī's works were established (Appendix C), and the place of Māwardī's *Statutes of Government* in Islamic history was indicated in a preliminary sketch (Appendix A).

In conclusion, the Islamic heritage of political thought was related to the Western political heritage by a comparison not with the political thought of the polis of classical antiquity or the nation-state of modern Europe but with the kindred heritage of medieval Christendom.

PART ONE
Reason and Revelation

1
Before Māwardī

Within an Islamic context, does reason have any role in arriving at the truth? If so, what is the relation of such truth to the truth of the Islamic revelation?[5]

Such questions are meaningless to philosophic nihilists to whom there is no truth; to sceptics who hold that whether there be truth or not man is incapable of arriving at it; and to relativists to whom truth is never absolute but is relative to an individual's belief or preference. Such intellectual positions, not unknown to the Islamic world, and usually attributed to the sophists,[6] are the very antithesis of normative social and political thought which has always concerned itself with norms that would serve the important sociopolitical function of limiting varying individual preferences.

The question of the relation of reason to revelation would also be meaningless to those who do not grant the validity of revelation. Almost all inhabitants of Muslim empires have accepted the validity of revelation – if not Muslim then Christian, Jewish or Zoroastrian. However, having expanded into the Indian subcontinent, Muslims came into contact with Buddhist and Hindu religions. To the latter they attribute the belief in the dispensability of revelation and the sufficiency of reason; to the former, the belief that truth is arrived at not through revelation or reason but through sense experience.[7]

Nobody can call himself a Muslim who does not accept as given God's revelation to Muḥammad. Such acceptance implies there could be no room for unbridled philosophical activities. Reason, if it has a place at all, must accommodate itself to revelation. This, however, can be done in many different ways. To set out briefly these various ways, indicating the degree of their dominance and the reasons for their success or failure, is essential for placing Māwardī's views in perspective.

The Muslim revelation served as the focus of a rapidly expanding community, and as an important integrative factor. As the movement of conquest spent its force and Muslim efforts turned to internal tasks – a development that I associate with the ʿAbbāsid revolution – internal conflicts expressed themselves in various interpretations of the Qur'ānic revelation. For revelation still to serve as an integrative force, a limit had to be put on varying interpretations.

Those concerned with the maintenance of political and social order were acutely aware of the need for limiting disputations in religion.

Thus Ibn al-Muqaffaʿ (d. 759), one of the earliest political thinkers in Islam, writes:

> The distinction between religion and human opinion is that religion is accepted on faith while the truth of human opinion is proved through disputation. He who makes religion the object of disputation would make religion a human opinion. He who makes religion a human opinion would become a legislator, and he who would legislate a religion unto himself has no religion.[8]

Ibn al-Muqaffaʿ is quick to realize that religion and human opinion cannot be neatly separated, for he adds 'Religion and human opinion might resemble each other in certain places. Had it not been for such resemblance, they would not have needed to be distinguished one from the other.'[9] Ibn al-Muqaffaʿ in fact accepts limited theological activity, primarily to prove the existence of God.[10]

The movement that aimed at supplying *the* interpretation under the ʿAbbāsids was the Muʿtazila. The Muʿtazila were by no means free thinkers. They accepted the Muslim revelation as given, and defended God, the source of revelation, and prophecy, the vehicle. They also attempted to interpret revelation allegorically to bring it in harmony with reason as far as possible. Muʿtazilite theology was eventually adopted by the Caliph Ma'mūn* (813–33) as the official doctrine. It is probably to serve the needs of the Muʿtazila that Ma'mūn encouraged extensive translations of Greek philosophical texts from Syriac and later directly from the Greek. The abandonment of Muʿtazilite theology by Mutawakkil (847–61) will be discussed in Part Two. Suffice it here to point out the inadequacy of such a rationalist theology as a mass ideology.

Speculative activity once accepted could not be limited to theological pursuits. The revival of the Hellenistic tradition gave rise to a philosophical movement known by its Greek name, Falsafa. While some philosophers were antagonistic to revelation, the majority did attempt an accommodation. These philosophers, however, let reason submerge revelation,[11] which they viewed as a somewhat crude yet useful way of addressing the common people whose intellect is limited.[12] The attitude of the Falāsifa towards men of religion is illustrated by al-Kindī (d. 870), the earliest philosopher, who insists that 'the human art that has the highest rank and the noblest position is the art

* Ma'mūn accepted from the Muʿtazila's ideas those which suited his political interests and cultural aspirations, for example the doctrine of the creation of the Qur'ān, but he did not accept their doctrine of free will.

of philosophy',[13] and then goes on to attack men of religion, arguing that their knowledge is inferior and their concern is to defend their positions and personal interests rather than the truth.[14] It is not surprising that the philosophers, by giving revelation a subordinate position and by their attitude of superiority,[15] arouse the hostility of jurists and theologians, who went to the extreme of accusing them of disbelief.

While individual philosophers presented no great political threat to the established order, philosophy became increasingly suspect as it came to be used by Ismā'īlis to underpin their revolutionary doctrines.[16] Hostility to philosophy increased further when the Ismā'īlis were able to found a rival empire with universalist claims – the Fāṭimids in Egypt (969). Ikhwān al-Ṣafā' (tenth century) attempted a marriage of reason and revelation that might be more popular than the strict philosophical attitude towards revelation.[17] While such an attempted synthesis has always found limited appeal among intellectuals, it never had a large following. That theology was more successful in defending revelation than philosophy was admitted even by some philosophers. For example, Abū Sulaymān al-Manṭiqī (tenth century) thinks that the efforts of the Ikhwān are misguided. Although he believes revelation to be either necessary or permitted by reason, he holds that 'Philosophy is true but it has nothing to do with revelation, and revelation is true but it has nothing to do with philosophy'.[18]

> Revelation is acquired from God, the Mighty the Exalted, through the intermediary of the messenger ... by means of inspiration, divine whispering, witnessing of signs and the appearance of miracles. ... Revelation includes matters that cannot be discussed or explored in depth. One must accept him who calls for these matters and points them out. Then 'Why' is voided, 'How' invalidated, 'Why not' ceases, and 'If' and 'Would that' are gone with the wind.[19]

That theological rather than philosophical speculation is more suited for defending revelation is argued in the following words: 'Religion is based on acceptance, assent and exaggerated exaltation, and has neither 'Why' nor 'How' except to the extent that religion is supported, its basis confirmed and evil attacks against it are refuted; for whatever exceeds this would weaken the root by raising doubt, and corrode the branch by arousing suspicion'.[20]

Mu'tazilism has laid down the basis of Muslim theology, and that was adopted by the 'Abbāsid Caliphs in the first half of the ninth century. It had a new lease on life in the second half of the tenth century, when it was championed by some of the Buwayhid princes outside Iraq. Part of the attraction of Muʿtazilism at this time is probably due to its usefulness in combating extreme Shīʿism,[21] which had become a serious threat with the rise of the Fāṭimids, and to its suitability as a bridge between Sunnism and the moderate Shīʿism of the Buwayhids. In the first half of the eleventh century, Muʿtazilism in Persia came under attack from east and west, from the expanding Ghaznawids (994–1040) who used the Sunnī banner and professed allegiance to the ʿAbbāsid Caliphs, and from the ʿAbbāsid Caliphs Qādir and Qā'im who attempted to reassert their authority vis-à-vis the Buwayhids.

Two important movements attempted to replace Muʿtazilism as the defenders of the faith, and found strong support in Baghdad, the seat of the caliphate. Both preferred to call their theology *uṣūl al-dīn*, roots of religion, rather than *kalām* which was identified with the Muʿtazila. These movements were Ashʿarism and Traditionalism. Ashʿarī and his followers[22] while using the methods of theology, de-emphasized the role of reason and emphasized God's omnipotence, incomprehensibility and the necessity of accepting many points of revelation on faith 'without asking how'. Even though Ashʿarī attempted to win over the Traditionalists by claiming to be a follower of Aḥmad Ibn Ḥanbal, the man who had challenged the Muʿtazila during the heyday of their power, the Ḥanbalites saw themselves as the rightful leaders of the Traditionalists, disapproved of theology even in its Ashʿarite form and developed their creed in the form of confessions of faith.[23] In Māwardī's time, the leader of the Ḥanbalites, Abū Yaʿlā, was forced to systematize the doctrines of his sect by writing on theology.[24] Interestingly enough, the result is not too far from Ashʿarite theology. In spite of such similarities, Ashʿarites and Ḥanbalites were antagonistic towards each other, the enmities often breaking out into violence in eleventh-century Baghdad. The Ḥanbalites were in a stronger position, for they were both a theological sect and a school of law. The Ashʿarites attempted to strengthen their position by identifying their theology with the well-established Shāfiʿite school of Law.[25]

At the same time that Ashʿarites and Traditionalists were engaged in subordinating reason to revelation, Ṣūfīs limited reason further by emphasizing religion as a personal experience and communion with the divine rather than an impersonal Law. The de-emphasis of the Law could have revolutionary implications. The insistence of Qushayrī, a contemporary of Māwardī, that Ṣūfī individualism must be balanced by a concept of authority – the authority of the Sufi Shaykh and of the Law – may be seen as an attempt to counteract such implications.[26]

2

Māwardī and After

How did Māwardī relate reason to revelation? Where does he fit within the continuum of positions described above? The latter question can be answered in general terms by saying that Māwardī's position was the middle road of the theologians. Unlike most Traditionalists and mystics, he felt that the learned may, indeed ought to, indulge in rational disputations to defend and elaborate God's revelation. He begins by asserting that reason is the basis of all knowledge,[27] but in fact if we are to follow his argument closely we find out that all he is saying is that reason is the basis of all proofs.[28] He makes the usual distinction between inborn and acquired knowledge. The former, needing no proof, is known either a priori, or through sense experience and unanimous assertion. It is the minimum knowledge that is prerequisite for legal responsibility. The latter is dependent on proofs and includes knowledge of the revealed Law, the validity of which depends on proofs of God and prophecy, the source and vehicle of revelation. He summarily dismisses those who claim to prove the existence of God through inspiration, on the grounds that it is purely subjective.

Māwardī argues that knowledge of God's existence can be arrived at through proof of the following three propositions:[29] the world is created and not eternal; the world has an eternal creator; and the creator is one and has no partners. The first proof that the world is created in time is based on the Aristotelian distinction between substance and accidents. Since accidents are created (for they cannot exist independently, and they alternate between existence and non-existence) then substance, which is inseparable from accidents, must also be created. The second proof that the world is created is its finitude. What is finite has a specific and determined size, which indicates that somebody must have specified and determined that size, and hence that it is created. Māwardī foresees the following possible objection: why cannot the substance of the world be uncreated as is the essence of God, and the accidents of the world created as are the actions of God? His answer is that the actions of God, because they occur in other than God, are separable from his essence, but the accidents of the world, because they occur in the world, are inseparable from its substance.

The demonstration that the world has an eternal creator is as follows: it is impossible that the world could have created itself, for this would imply that it existed before it was created. Whatever comes into existence must have its cause or agent, as, for example, the existence of a building would necessitate the existence of a builder. The creator of the world must be eternal, for otherwise he would have need for a creator, and so on ad infinitum.

Māwardī supports his proposition that God is one and has no partners in the following manner. The Creator's eternity implies an omnipotence and free will that are illustrated by the act of creating the world. The Creator's omnipotence means he can have no opposing partners and that he created not only a selected part but all of what is created. That is, there is no room for any other Creator. The unity of the Creator is further supported by an analogy between motion and creation. As a single motion can be the result of only one mover [sic], so one creation is the result of only one Creator.

Although Māwardī offers proofs of God's existence, he insists that God is known through 'rational necessity', by which he means that the outcome of the argument is never in question. While his proof of God's existence is not especially original,[30] his defence of prophecy is rather eloquent and has been considered by some Muslim writers as the best in this field.[31]

Māwardī's defence of Muḥammad's prophecy is directed against two groups: those who deny or limit Muḥammad's mission while accepting prophecy in general,[32] and those who deny prophecy altogether.[33] Among the former group are the Jews, who, according to Māwardī, based their denial of Muḥammad's prophecy on the rejection of the Muslim view that each revelation abrogates those that preceded it. Some Jews argue against abrogation on rational grounds, claiming that it would imply fickleness on the part of God. Māwardī's answer is that abrogation is a sign not of God's fickleness, but of his free will[34] or of his consideration for what is best[35] for man at any given time; abrogation is analogous to God's enrichment of the poor and impoverishment of the rich, and does not deny His wisdom. Other Jews simply support their rejection of the principle of abrogation by Biblical reference. Māwardī replies that 'Moses had abrogated the revelation of those prophets who preceded him'. As examples, Biblical episodes are recalled in which 'Adam gave his daughters in marriage to his sons; Jacob sanctioned man's marriage to two sisters at the same time; Abraham married his brother's daughter[36] ... Since all these practices were annulled by Moses in accordance with his law, Mosaic law may, therefore, be abrogated by subsequent revelation'.[37] Against those who do not deny prophecy but hold that Muḥammad was sent only to the Arabs, or only to the pagans, the argument contends that acceptance of Muḥammad's prophethood even to a limited group assumes his truthfulness and, since he claimed to be sent to all mankind, the universality of his mission.

In answer to those who accept the principle of prophecy, but contend that Muḥammad performed no convincing miracles, the greatest part of *Aʿlām al-nubuwwa* was devoted to an enumeration and classification of Muḥammad's miracles, with particular emphasis on the miracle par excellence, the Qur'ān.

Māwardī divides those who deny prophecy altogether into three groups: heretical, atheistic materialists; monotheistic Brahmins; and the Falāsifa. His arguments are directed only against the last two groups, who grant the essential premise of God's existence. He bases his accusation against the Falāsifa, who 'outwardly do not pretend to deny prophecy', on their teaching that religious sciences are secondary to philosophical sciences. Denial of prophecy is attacked first by stating the reasons for such denial and then offering suitable refutation of these reasons. For example, against the contention that miracles, the basic proof of prophecy, are no more than the hocus-pocus of swindlers and magicians, Māwardī argues that miracles are quite different from the magicians' tricks. The latter deceive only the ignorant and gullible and can be taught and imitated, while the former baffle even men of intelligence and can be neither learned nor duplicated.

Others reject prophecy, claiming that the various so-called prophets are contradictory while intellectual matters are not. Māwardī replies that the various revelations do not differ in essential matters such as the unity of God and his attributes, and may differ only in regard to religious observances. These differences are not all contradictory; and those that seem so are explained away by the need of changing times in accordance with either God's will or man's best interest. Moreover, just as the authority of the intellect is not vitiated even though men of intelligence may differ on intellectual matters, similarly the authority of prophets cannot be rejected even though prophets may differ on certain aspects of revelation.

The answer to those who claim that prophecy is contradictory to reason is the affirmation that revelation is never inconsistent with reason. All that revelation requires is either permitted or required by reason. In the former case, reason is augmented, and in the latter, confirmed by revelation.[38]

Even if revelation is consistent with reason, it may still be asked: why is revelation necessary? Is not reason sufficient for the ordering of man's life? Even if religion is necessary, must it be based on revelation? Māwardī's answer to the last question is simply a statement of his view that no religion is valid without 'messengers who convey what God – may he be exalted – requires'.[39] It, therefore, should be borne in mind that when Māwardī speaks of religion, he means revealed religion.

In meeting the arguments of those who consider reason sufficient and revelation dispensable – a view that he attributes to the Brahmins[40] – Māwardī does not allow himself to be forced to the other extreme of dismissing reason altogether. He contests not the usefulness but the sufficiency of reason.

Māwardī asserts that 'reason necessitates religion',[41] 'for reason forbids that men be set free and forsaken; that they depend on their differing opinions and divergent passions; because such a situation would lead to disagreement and conflict and would result in the severance of mutual relations. Therefore, men cannot dispense with a religion on which they agree and through which they are brought together.'[42]

Three points are implicit in this stand: a consensus is an indispensable basis of any community; the intellect cannot provide this consensus; and consensus, to be effective, must be transcendentally based. In support of his view that reason cannot lead to agreement, it is pointed out that intellectual proofs which are equally sound can lead to differing conclusions.[43] The implication that the consensus must be based on religion is explicitly defended in these words: 'Because men's intellects would often disdain to agree with their equals or to follow them, men cannot be brought together except by obeying God through obeying what his messengers have transmitted'.[44]

Reason is not only inadequate as a basis for consensus, but it is also insufficient as a restraint. Only religion can 'reform the heart's evil inclinations, lead to friendliness and equitable behaviour, and induce harmony and mutual affection'.[45]

Why cannot reason perform these functions? Māwardī's answer – a corollary of his psychology that sees all human actions as stemming from desire for rewards or fear of punishment[46] – is that the most effective incentives for doing good and desisting from evil, desire of heaven and fear of hell,[47] lie outside the scope of reason.[48]

In addition, religion is indispensable as a basis for a law that produces harmony by bridging the gap between extremes of power and status. 'Through reason, men cannot agree upon a rule of law before which the weak is equal to the strong, the noble to the humble.'[49] Though Māwardī, in demonstrating the need for religion, focuses primarily on the community, he does not lose sight of the individual altogether, but is aware of the importance of religion to the individual not only as a restraint but also as a 'solace for the soul in its misfortune'.[50]

In the light of the above discussion, it is now possible to ascertain Māwardī's exact theological position. He has been described by some as a Muʿtazilite,[51] and by others as an Ashʿarite.[52] In fact he was neither. He did not profess to be a Muʿtazilite[53] or an Ashʿarite, nor is he so considered by either sect.[54] He was an independent thinker who refused to follow blindly any one theological sect.[55] Māwardī declared himself against the Muʿtazila on the sensitive question of the creation of the Qur'ān,[56] upon which popular antagonism against the Muʿtazila was always centred, but held firm to a rationalist theology that saw the spheres of reason and revelation as overlapping rather than mutually exclusive. He agrees with the Muʿtazilites that God takes man's best interest into account and would not demand in His revelation what is impossible.[57] The Ashʿarites, on the other hand, reject these views as human limitations on God's free will: nothing is incumbent upon God; He does not have to take man's interest into account and may demand the impossible.[58] Another Muʿtazilite principle, upon which Qur'ānic exegesis was based, is to interpret God's commands (i.e. the text of the Qur'ān) in accordance with His will. The Ashʿarites reacted against the Muʿtazilites by divorcing God's commands from His will. Māwardī, on the other hand, starting with the Muʿtazilite concept of a rationally comprehensible God, insists that God's commands and will are in absolute harmony, but unlike the Muʿtazila he holds that the commands (i.e. the text of the Qur'ān) must be the starting point: it is God's commands in the Qur'ān that make known to us His will, and not what we postulate to be His will that gives validity to a given interpretation of His commands. Even though Māwardī as a Shāfiʿite accepts Qur'ān, tradition, consensus and analogy as the principles for deduction of the Law, he, unlike Ashʿarites and Traditionalists, does not divorce the Law from reason, but holds that agreement with reason is a condition of the validity of the Law.[59] Since God's commands and prohibitions do not encompass all men's actions, Māwardī advocates that reason be followed in such cases. Even the possibility that ordinances based only on reason may be included in the Muslim system of Law is not denied!

Māwardī was a harmonizer who refrained from polemical attacks except against the most extreme, for example Bātinis.[60] As a jurist he was primarily concerned with concrete formulation of positive Law in regard to which the differences among rival tendencies were relatively minor when compared with the polarization of abstract theological positions.[61]

Such a relatively independent mind did enable Māwardī to write the first Muslim book on public Law. However, his rationalist theology was never very popular in the following centuries. Just as the individual was subordinated psychologically and socially to the authority of the group, individual reason was also subordinated to the authority of Muḥammad's traditions or the Ṣūfī Shaykh. In theological circles, Traditionalist theology and Ashʿarite occasionalism were always more popular than Māwardī's rationalism. Even Falsafa, the bastion of rationalism, gave way to theosophy which attempted to combine syllogistic proofs with intuitive knowledge.[62] An anti-rationalist orientation did provide the Muslim world with a limited measure of stability, but did not prepare it to meet the challenge of a modernized West – a challenge that Muslims have yet to comprehend in spite of its dramatic political manifestations.

PART TWO
Politics and Revelation

3

Legal Criterion

Before Māwardī

Islam makes no sharp distinction between the spiritual and temporal. It concerns itself with all aspects of life, including politics. This total claim of Islam is related to the historical fact that Muḥammad was both a prophet and statesman, and his revealed message spread not in antagonism to a hostile political order but as the banner of a new and rapidly expanding empire.

The relation of ideology to power was not very problematic to the Muslim community at Medina, because Muḥammad combined in his person both rulership and prophecy. With the death of Muḥammad, the new religious leadership naturally laid claim to political leadership as well. Such a claim, made good by the first two caliphs who enjoyed great prestige, became increasingly difficult to assert within the context of imperial expansion.

The success of the Arab conquest was due to the unifying banner of Islam, the fighting power of the Arab tribes, and the capable leadership of the Meccan aristocracy. The new religious leadership, the old aristocracy and the tribes did not always have the same interests and goals, and conflict was inherent in their alliance.

The ascendancy of the Meccan aristocracy, under Uthmān, antagonized the tribes and led to his murder and the first civil war. Religious sentiment which centred around ʿAlī tacitly accepted the tribal rebellion but, suspicious of the anarchic tendencies of the tribes, eventually acquiesced in the ascendancy of Muʿāwiya – a member of the old aristocracy – as the best guarantee of peace and order. Acceptance of Muʿāwiya's triumph is the political essence of the Murji'a[63] theological sect, which flourished under the Umayyids.

The Umayyids essentially perpetuated the imperial system that they inherited from the Byzantine and Sassanid predecessors. As long as the Arab tribes provided the military basis of the empire, identified themselves exclusively with Islam, and reaped the benefits of a continuous expansion of empire, the problem of legitimization of the rulers was not acute. The spread of Islam among non-Arabs, the attractiveness of settled life in garrison cities that became thriving commercial centres, and the shifting of the focus of conquest to the eastern front undermined the basis of Umayyid rule and culminated in the ʿAbbāsid revolution.

Under the Umayyids, many opponents of the government, including those who saw too great a gap between the religious ideal and political realities, had tended to view themselves as the party (Shīʿa) of ʿAlī, symbol of the earliest opposition to Umayyid ascendancy. The Shīʿīs were an important factor in the ʿAbbāsid revolution.

The ʿAbbāsids, using the banner of Islam, aroused great hopes and united many elements that had little in common save opposition to the status quo. As is often the case with revolutions, the problem of constructing a new order proved to be a far more demanding task than destroying the old. The problems of consolidation were the more pressing because the distracting movement of expansion had by then spent its force.

Faced with these problems, the ʿAbbāsids consciously utilized religious ideology as a basis of legitimization of their rule and as a unifying force in the Muslim community. One of the first writers to discuss the growing tension between the realities of ʿAbbāsid politics and the ideals of the Muslim revelation was Ibn al-Muqaffaʿ (d. 759). His description of 'religious dominion', wherein the ruler ensures obedience of the people by establishing their religion which defines their rights and obligations,[64] fits very well the Muslim ideal according to which obedience is due to God and His Law and not to the ruler's will. This principle, formulated in the prophetic tradition 'No obedience is due to any creature in disobeying the Creator', was used by enemies of the ʿAbbāsid dynasty as a justification of their opposition. While some supporters of the regime reacted in an extreme manner and demanded absolute submission to the ruler, Ibn al-Muqaffaʿ shrewdly accepted the above tradition, but interpreted it in such a way as to empty it of any revolutionary content. Obedience to God means that the ruler may not contravene God's commands such as prayer, fasting and pilgrimage. As far as government is concerned, for example the conduct of financial and military affairs, the execution of legal ordinances, and rule in accordance with personal opinion when there is no prophetic tradition, this is the exclusive right of the imām, and the people have no rights whatsoever.[65] Ibn al-Muqaffaʿ further recommends that the ruler produce a unified code of religious law by exercising his individual judgment to decide on questions upon which the jurists disagree. Starting from a hierarchic view of society, Ibn al-Muqaffaʿ advocates the ideal of a powerful imām enjoying the support of a privileged elite, of wealth, power and religion, and ruling with benevolence and justice towards all. This would correspond to his second type of dominion, 'rule by strength and resolution'.[66] He concedes that this would engender opposition, but he assures us that attacks on the lowly would not be harmful given the support of the strong.

The tension to which Ibn al-Muqaffaʿ addressed himself can be seen sociologically as the tension between the rulers and the various other groups which embodied their particular interests and visions of the future in differing interpretations of revelation. Let us look at some of these groups.

The Shīʿīs hoped to resolve this tension by having an all-powerful imām descendant of the line of ʿAlī, who, enjoying divine guidance, inherits the function of the prophet in religion as well as politics. Such a position, putting no stock in numbers but leaving religious as well as political guidance to an infallible imām, serves very well as the banner of disgruntled minorities, who cannot claim the legitimacy of numbers in their opposition to the ʿAbbāsid victors.

It seems to me that, after the ʿAbbāsid revolution, the political significance of the Muʿtazila lies in its opposition to the revolutionary implications of the Shīʿīs and weaning them away from the extremist Ismāʿīlīs.

The Muʿtazila's vision of an alliance of the religiously learned with the ruler was much closer to ʿAbbāsid realities. It was not surprising that the ʿAbbāsid caliphs eventually went as far as imposing the Muʿtazilite position as the 'official interpretation'. What is the significance of the fall of the Muʿtazila from grace after three and a half decades? Professor Gibb's conclusion that this 'proved once and for all that the religious institution of Islam was independent of the caliphate or any other political institution'[67] needs modification. It is my view that Muʿtazilism, in spite of its developed polemics in defence of the ʿAbbāsids against extreme opposition, was too intellectual to serve as an adequate mass ideology. The government eventually found support in two important developments that could rally a wider following than the Muʿtazila.

First, a large segment of Shiʿis, while insisting that the present political situation was far from ideal, adopted a quietist attitude, pushing fulfilment into the eschatological future, when the *mahdī* would appear and fill the earth with justice. This trend culminated in Twelver Shīʿism.

Second, increased activity in the development of *fiqh* and *ḥadīth* culminated in the crystallization of the principal Law schools by the middle of the ninth century and the main collections of *ḥadīth* by the end of the same century. It is true that the rulers did not arrogate to themselves, as Ibn al-Muqaffaʿ would have liked, the exclusive right to develop and codify either Law or Traditions. However, to see the *ʿulamā'* as arriving at consensus through independent activity would be an exaggeration. Examination of the Law books and the 'six books' of *ḥadīth* reveals a striking neglect of government beyond certain general principles: the caliph must be a Qurayshite; he holds the flock in trust; his responsibility is very grave but he is answerable only to God in the hereafter; the flock must carry out its duty and obey even though the ruler might not fulfil his duties. Even Abū Yūsuf, who in the introduction to his book on land tax concerned himself with the Muslim principles of government, is hardly aware of the requirements of politics. He advocates that the ruler should put the affairs of the hereafter before the affairs of the world.[68] This is hardly adequate counsel to a man who is primarily entrusted with dealing with this world and would surely lead to ruin, as the fourteenth-century sultan Ibn Ziyān rightly observes.[69] Is it an accident that the 'six books' of *ḥadīth* advocate quietism at a time when *ḥadīth*s were circulated in favour of all kinds of positions including the right of rebellion?[70] Would it not be reasonable to postulate implicit and tacit support of the authorities to jurists and collectors of the 'six books' of *ḥadīth*?

The religious 'institution' was not as independent of the government as Professor Gibb implies. Men of religion were limited most strikingly in the field of politics, and the caliphs continued their effort to impose particular religious positions. Qādir's and Qā'im's (first half of the eleventh century) support of the quietist Traditionalists and the persecution of the Muʿtazila is no less of an interference in the religious 'institution' than Ma'mūn's support of the Muʿtazila.

Quite early in the ʿAbbāsid period, the learned were aware of the great gap between the Islamic political ideal of a rule of Law and the facts of political life. The learned had a free hand in the elaboration of the Law, but their formulation, while rejecting Ibn al-Muqaffaʿ's rigidly hierarchic view of society, had relatively little to say about the constitution of government. This awareness of the fact that the elaborated *sharīʿa* did not cover all aspects of life, including politics, was rationalized in two ways: fulfilment was pushed back into the past, hence the myth of the golden age of the rightly-guided Caliphs (al-Rāshidun al-Mahdiyyūn), or to the future, hence the widespread belief in the *mahdī* who would appear at the end of time and restore justice.

The fact that the *sharīʿa* as formulated by the schools of Law was not all-inclusive led many political thinkers to introduce an extra religious criterion as a guide to governmental action. For example, Ibn Abī al-Rabīʿ, writing in the middle of the ninth century,[71] lays down as guides to the ruler not only prophetic Law but also divine wisdom and the precepts of reason.[72]

Abū Sulaymān al-Manṭiqī, in the second half of the tenth century, accepts the Muslim ideal as expressed by Abū Yūsuf that government should be conducted in accordance with religious traditions, but he hastens to add 'insofar as practicable'. When the religious ideology proves inadequate, the ruler must follow the rules of government as spelled out, for example, by the philosophers in books on politics. He warns the ruler against disregarding the rules of the world as well as religion, for political affairs are inextricably bound with both.[73]

The caliphs' power reached its lowest in the middle of the tenth century. This historical position is described most clearly by Māwardī's contemporary Bīrūnī (d. 1043), who sees the development of dual leadership: political and religious.[74] Those who accepted this duality as legitimate (e.g. Māwardī's older contemporary, Tawhīdī, who considers the prince as deriving his sanction directly from God)[75] often failed to deal with the crucial problem of the relation of political to religious leadership. Ikhwān al-Ṣafā', a philosophical reformist movement of the latter part of the tenth century, did concern itself with this problematic relation. What were the results?

The Ikhwān held that the various Muslim rulers were the inheritors only of Muḥammad's political or royal function. The true inheritors of Muhammad's religious or prophetic functions are neither the rulers nor the *ʿulamā'* but are the philosophers who are versed in revelation – Muslim, Jewish and Christian.[76] In addressing themselves to this duality, the Ikhwān end up with a monistic solution. True to their Platonic legacy they advocate that the philosophers must become kings,[77] but only after they have spread their teachings, especially among intellectuals and Shīʿīs.[78] While such an intellectual ideal was never fulfilled, the related Ismāʿīlī teachings, more hierarchic and authoritarian, found partial fulfilment in the Fāṭimid empire, in the tenth to the twelth centuries.

The above discussion has shown how the early jurists tended to neglect the area of politics, and how political thinkers consequently attempted to supplement the *sharīʿa* by an extralegal criterion. It was left to Māwardī, an eminent jurist, a *mujtahid* rather than *muqallid*,[79] to attempt to include politics in the sharīʿa. Feeling that his predecessors had not paid enough attention to public law,[80] he set for himself the task of summarizing the relevant positions of the jurists and systematically expanding and supplementing their deductions in accordance with the accepted principles of jurisprudence, hence, *al-Aḥkām al-sulṭāniyya*, which is to my knowledge the first Muslim attempt at a detailed deduction of the elements of Law that pertain to government.[81] What were the results of Māwardī's efforts to include government under the *sharīʿa*?[82]

4

Legal Criterion

Māwardī and After

Even though he does not believe that man's perfection is to be attained in this world, Māwardī does concern himself with government, for he considers this world a necessary preparatory stage for the hereafter.[83] While on this earth, a man cannot live alone, for God made him such that 'he needs others of his kind'.[84] Yet human cooperation is greatly hampered by man's powerful and insidious passions. 'There is in the nature of man a love of competition and contention for that which he prefers, and a desire for subduing those whom he opposes, such that he is not restrained except by a powerful and persistent deterrent.'[85] God has given man reason and revelation, which, though adequate as a guide, are insufficient as a restraint – hence the need for a ruling power. 'Through awe of it, divergent passions are brought closer together and agreement is produced; due to its power various contentions for superiority are restrained; and out of fear of it, those who are at enmity are subdued.'[86] A ruling power is the most effective restraint, 'for reason and religion are often weak and overcome by passion'.[87]

Power cannot last unless it is based on religion. 'Some kings have often neglected religion and relied in the management of their affairs on their might and the great number of their soldiery, not realizing that their soldiery, when they do not believe in obedience as a religious duty, would be more harmful than any adversary.'[88] Power, if it is not based on religion, 'will neither endure nor will its days be cloudless'.[89]

Conversely, power is needed for

> the guardianship and protection of religion, refutation of false beliefs, guarding against any change in religion, admonishing those who deviate from the faith to return to it, and chiding those who stubbornly persist in their error or act perversely. If these matters are not severed from it by a strong ruling power and adequate care, religion is changed and distorted by those who hold false and deviating opinions. There never has been a religion whose ruling power perished but that its precepts changed and it became extinct, with every leader offering his innovation, and every era contributing further to its decline.[90]

Even if it endured for a while, power that is divorced from religion is still illegitimate. 'Any power that is not based on religion which creates a consensus so that people will consider obedience a duty and cooperation an obligation ... is an oppressive and corrupting power.'[91] Māwardī goes on to say that power, the necessary guardian of religion, must be exercised in accordance with religious ordinances and tradition.[92]

Here is seemingly an expression, in general terms, of the Muslim concept of authority: power,to be legitimate, must be based on religion

To understand the content and ramifications of this view, one must examine what it in fact entails. A logical starting point is to ask how power is to be constituted if based on religion.

Māwardī's answer is cast in traditional Islamic terms, and thus revolves, at least as far as its formal structure is concerned, around the 'institution' of the imāma[93] from which emanate directly or indirectly all appointments to governmental functions. The imāma,[94] vicegerency of the prophet, not of God,[95] in the protection of religion and the government of the world, is obligatory[96] through *ijmāʿ* (consensus).[97] Though it is not explicitly stated,[98] the basis of *ijmāʿ*, as may be deduced from Māwardī's views expressed elsewhere,[99] is both reason and revelation.[100]

The office of the imāma can be filled only through a contract[101] voluntarily concluded between the electors (who must be religious, learned and wise) and a Qurayshite of sound mind and body who in addition to being courageous and wise must possess probity and the learning necessary for *ijtihād*.[102] The crucial question arises around who may act as electors. On the basis of *ijmāʿ*, Māwardī endorses the historical precedent that the existing caliph may designate his successor.[103] He is thus led logically to a tacit acceptance of the doctrine that the contract of the imāma is valid even if made by a single qualified elector.[104]

Does not this position empty the idea of contract of all political content? Why does Māwardī insist on election even though it be by only one qualified elector? Would it not be less hypocritical to accept, as the Ḥanbalites frankly do, an imāma acquired by force?[105] Three important points lie behind Māwardī's dogged adherence to seemingly legal formalism.

First, within the context of polemical writings on the imāma, the principle of election (*ikhtiyār*) essentially means rejection of the opposing Shīʿī principle of divine designation (naṣṣ).

Second, though he might acquire his position through the preponderance of his power, the imām has to fulfil minimum conditions of which the learned are the only proper judge.

Third, the imām, by entering into contract with even a single representative of the religious Law, pledges himself to uphold this Law, which is the ideal constitution of the Muslim community.

If the essence of contract is a pledge by one who already has power, to act in accordance with the Law, then discussion of legitimacy would have to shift to the acts of the ruler. According to Māwardī, a ruler would attain legitimacy, i.e. rendering obedience to him becomes obligatory, only when he carries out his duties in accordance with God's Law.

Māwardī was acutely aware of the fact that the specific formulations of God's Law in the *sharīʿa* have tended to neglect government. Principles of government and administration were usually discussed and elaborated in *adab*[106] works that had their roots in the Byzantine and, more importantly, the Sassanid tradition. This indebtedness was openly acknowledged by Muslim writers. For example, the author of *al-Tāj* (*The Crown*) wrote: 'And it is from them [non-Arab kings] that we have taken the principles of kingship ...'.[107] Māwardī himself recognized his debt to his predecessors. In the introduction to his *Tashīl al-naẓar*, he wrote: 'I have summarized in this book the precepts of government that have been masterfully laid down by the ancients'.[108] But Māwardī was not a mere summarizer, for he goes on to say: 'Previous works are not an adequate substitute for a book that in clarifying the requirements of divine Law and the well-known principles of government conforms with religion and the world'.[109]

Māwardī's principal concern in most of his political writings is to expand divine Law to include governmental action, or at least to ensure that government is not divorced from the spirit of divine Law. According to Māwardī, fulfilling God's law involves carrying out a number of duties. In general terms, the religious duty of the ruler is to maintain Islam in accordance with its fixed principles and the established consensus. The fundamental requirements of the Islamic religion being belief in God and the mission of Muḥammad, the concrete duties of the ruler are to safeguard against renunciation of the faith or extreme deviation from its doctrines. The regulations applying to one who renounces Islam are very simple and unequivocal: an apostate, if he refuses to repent, is punishable by death, and his property accrues to the treasury.[110]

As far as deviation on specific points of belief is concerned, great tolerance is shown, as long as Muslims perform their prescribed religious duties and render obedience to the imām: 'When a party of Muslims deviate from the right path, dissent from the opinion of the community, and embrace a new doctrine that they have invented', then the following cases may be distinguished:

> If they do not openly renounce their obedience to the imām nor isolate themselves in any given locality, but are dispersed such that they can be easily dealt with, they should be left alone, combat should not be waged against them, and the rules of justice pertaining to their rights and responsibilities under the Law are applied to them. But if while mingled with the 'orthodox' they flaunt their doctrines, then the imām must make clear to them the falsity of their belief and the invalidity of their innovation, so that they will forsake them for the right belief and agreement with the community; and he may curb those individuals who make show of their false beliefs by reprimanding them and employing disciplinary punishment, but he may not exceed these measures by imposing death or ḥudūd[111] penalties.

Even 'if such a deviating party dissociate themselves from the orthodox and isolate themselves in a given locality in which they set themselves apart from the community, ... they may not be fought as long as they do not neglect their religious duties or renounce obedience [to the imām]'.[112] This formulation accommodates to the ʿAbbāsid caliphate various dissident groups of which the most important were those Shīʿīs who gave nominal allegiance to the ʿAbbāsid caliph.

However, if the deviating party renounce obedience to the imām, it is necessary that war be waged against them. This stand, consistent with the position that the community may have only one imām at a given time,[113] is apparently based more on political than religious considerations. For while a dissenting imām (e.g. Fāṭimid) must be fought, his existence is deemed essential to, and does validate, the performance of religious duties by his subjects.[114]

As to the policy that the ruler should follow when faced with great religious dissension among the flock, it is recommended that he concern himself with religious learning and seek the help of the *ʿulamā'* to arrive at correct beliefs and combat falsehood. Conscious of the impracticality of reaching a religious consensus after long-standing disagreement, Māwardī recommends that the ruler emphasize points upon which his flock does agree, utilizing prophetic traditions and Qur'ānic verses that call for unity, and de-emphasizing questions upon which unanimity is not likely be reached.

In addition to profession of the faith, the pillars of Islam are prayer, fast, alms and pilgrimage. What are the ruler's duties in regard to these religious obligations? The ruler must appoint a *muḥtasib* (agoranomos) who, as part of his responsibility to command people to do good and desist from evil, would see to the proper observance of the Friday prayers, and would check the public and unexcused disregard of the

Ramadan fast. Infraction of the Law in these areas is to be checked also by the official in charge of the redress of wrongs. The appointment of imāms to lead the faithful in prayer is the right of the local communities of believers. The ruler is permitted to appoint imāms only to mosques that are maintained by him. Māwardī, as a Shāfiʿite, disagrees with Abū Ḥanīfa and the people of Iraq, who hold that the validity of the Friday prayer is dependent on the appointment of the imām by the caliph.

The religious duty of the ruler is not only to protect religion but also to expand it. He should wage holy war against those who, having been invited, refuse to embrace Islam until they convert or accept Dhimmī[115] status. The crux of Islam, however, is its system of law; and the religious duty of the ruler is essentially to see to its proper administration. It is therefore natural that in Māwardī's important work, *al-Aḥkām al-sulṭaniyya*, the administration of justice is given considerable attention.[116]

Just as the *sharīʿa* is theoretically the only law of the Muslim community, the *qāḍī* is ideally the sole judicial arm of the *sharīʿa*. Like other bureaucrats, he is appointed either directly by the caliph or by one to whom the caliph has delegated his authority. The function of the *qāḍī* is considered of such importance that the inhabitants of a given area are permitted, in the absence of a caliph, to appoint their own judge; however, when a new caliph is recognized, the *qāḍī* must receive confirmation by the caliph. *Qāḍī*s may appoint their own deputies and may hold other offices at the same time.

The conditions prerequisite for a judge (*qāḍī*) are that he be a free,[117] adult, male[118] Muslim[119] possessing reason,[120] probity,[121] sound hearing and sight, and knowledge of the Law. Māwardī dwells on the last condition, knowledge of the Law, including, in his judgment, knowledge of the principles of jurisprudence as well as positive Law. Only a *mujtahid*, that is one who knows the principles of jurisprudence, may be appointed judge or *muftī*.[122] Knowledge of the principles of jurisprudence refers specifically to:

- knowledge of the Qur'ān, its various ordinances, whether they are abrogating or abrogated, clear or ambiguous, unlimited or limited, general or explicit;
- knowledge of the established traditions (both sayings and deed) of the Prophet, including the ability to discern whether a given tradition is sound or not, whether it is transmitted through unanimous assertion or individual report,[123] and whether its reference is specific or general;
- knowledge of the interpretations of his predecessors, so that he will follow those interpretations in regard to which consensus has been

established, and to use his individual judgment in such places where no consensus exists;

- knowledge of analogy, necessary for relating questions of positive Law that have not been provided for to fundamental principles that are explicitly stated and unanimously accepted.

The jurisdiction of the *qāḍīs*, contrary to the Muslim ideal, was by no means all-inclusive. Māwardī is willing to concede that the jurisdiction of an individual judge may be limited (e.g. to a certain time, locality, litigants, or subject matter), but he insists on the *qāḍī*'s right to use his independent judgment and not to be limited to following a single school of Law. The exercise of independent judgment is not only a right but also a duty. Therefore, Māwardī opposes the appointment as *qāḍīs* of those who deny the value of analogy,[124] follow the letter of the text and accept the opinion of their predecessors where the text makes no provision, but reject individual interpretation and shun reflection and inference.

Conceding the fact that the *qāḍīs* were not the only judicial officials in Islam, Māwardī devotes himself to a definition of supplementary jurisdictions in an attempt to limit deviation from the *sharīʿa*. Māwardī accepts the *maẓālim* jurisdiction to deal with cases where the ordinary judge is helpless in the face of the great power of the litigants and to redress the wrongs of the mighty, especially the civil and military bureaucracy. This does not mean that ordinary justice is to be disregarded. The *maẓālim* is a compromise combining the power of the rulership with the equity of the judicature. Māwardī concedes that a *maẓālim* official, unlike an ordinary judge, is not restricted to approved witnesses; has the power of investigation, for which purpose he may recess a case; does not need the consent of the two parties before referring a dispute for settlement by conciliation; and may use intimidation, place under arrest or require bail. However, Māwardī insists that as far as handing down judgments is concerned, a *maẓālim* official must adhere strictly to the requirements of the Law as would any ordinary judge. 'It often happens that *maẓālim* officials, misconstruing their jurisdiction, act unjustly and overstep their proper limits.'

In discussing *ḥisba* (supervision of markets and morals), Māwardī argues that it is an executive rather than judicial office. The *muḥtasib* is conceded the right of making decisions based on customary practice, but not on divine Law. This is strictly the province of the *qāḍī*. The *muḥtasib*'s function is seen to be essentially the same as that of his forerunner, the ancient agoranomos. While he may handle cases involving short weight or measure, fraudulent sales, and default on payment by those who are able, the *muḥtasib* may not adjudicate, for he is not empowered to hear testimony or swear in litigants.

In discussing criminal law, which was usually outside the jurisdiction of ordinary judges, an attempt is again made to define the jurisdiction of the executive. An executive official[125] may handle cases of criminal assault even if they do not entail legal punishment or fine. He is given great leeway in investigating a case on his own, taking into account the character and the record of the accused, exacting oaths, a hearing testimony, even from a non-Muslim. He may use threats and intimidation, and may imprison the accused pending investigation. Māwardī finds himself compelled to grant that a governor, when he has a strong suspicion that the accusation is true, may inflict the persuasion that he feels necessary to lead the accused to tell the truth.[126] However, Māwardī insists that in the determination of legal penalties once the guilt of the criminal has been established, the executive is as bound by the Law as any ordinary judge.[127]

In addition to the above religious and legal responsibilities, the ruler had to fulfil additional duties that are of the essence of all government. These duties are essentially the provision of internal and external security, which call for the maintenance of a civil and military bureaucracy. The proper relation of the bureaucracy to the flock is described as in previous empires by the word 'justice' (*'adl*), to which we will return in the following section. It is significant that Māwardī, in discussing government, always used the criterion of justice in addition to religion. Not only does he use this additional criterion, but he also attempts to give it religious sanction by giving it special emphasis even in his book on divine Law.[128]

The essence of Māwardī's thought is aimed at the fulfilment of the requirements of religion and justice, by those who are properly qualified, with little regard for constitutional organization. This is not to say that he neglects constitutional organization altogether. The fulfilment of the religious function necessitates maintenance of the caliphate as the head of the religious institution, and the symbol of the unity of the community and the prevalence of religion.

This generalization can be illustrated by noting the way in which Māwardī dealt with the power realities of his time. The first political reality was that the imām who was supposed to be in direct charge of the administration had usually relinquished such responsibility to his *wazīr*. Māwardī deals with the wazīrate at length. In addition to the chapter in the *Aḥkām*, he devotes a separate book to the rules of the wazīrate. The special attention is probably related to the revival of the office of the caliph's *wazīr* by the caliph Qā'im as part of his attempt to assert his authority vis-à-vis declining Buwayhid power.

That the caliph needed and had the right to delegate his authority is the basic organizational principle of Muslim government, and as such was not contested. While accepting current practices and principles, Māwardī attempts to limit extreme reliance on delegation of the imām's responsibility. He distinguishes between two types of *wazīrs*: *wazīr tafwīḍ*, enjoying delegated authority, and *wazīr tanfīdh*, limited to the execution of the imām's policies. He sees the benefit of appointing *wazīrs* of the latter type, possessing no power to act as judges, appoint administrators, or formulate financial or military policy.[129] But he considers appointment of the former type the usual Muslim practice, as resignation of authority.[130]

A *wazīr tafwīḍ*, since he is to exercise almost as much authority as the caliph, must meet all the conditions necessary for the election of the caliph except for descent from Quraysh. Moreover, he must be competent in military and financial affairs for which he is responsible. Lest the *wazīr* be as powerful as the caliph, Māwardī insists that the *wazīr* must keep the imām informed of administrative measures and various appointments, and the imām should review the work of the *wazīr* with an eye to confirming or revoking it. The *wazīr* has the same powers as the imām except designating a successor, resigning, or dismissing an appointee of the imām. Obviously the *wazīr* could not carry out his duties properly if his every act could be revoked from above. Therefore, the imām, while he may reverse questions of policy or appointments, is not empowered to revoke any of the acts of the *wazīr* that conform to the Law.

A second political reality was the actual position held by the caliphs. Supposed to be supreme political figures, for 100 years they had been virtual prisoners of the Shīʿī Buwayhid princes. This situation is what Māwardī calls curtailment of liberty and arises when control of the imām is seized by one of his auxiliaries who arrogates to himself the execution of affairs, without openly showing disobedience or publicly declaring opposition. According to Māwardī, such a situation would not invalidate the imāma. In other words, the minimum constitutional requirement for the validity of the imāma is holding the nominal allegiance of those in actual power.

But are those who by virtue of superior force have seized control over the imām to be considered legitimate merely by paying their nominal allegiance to the caliph? Here, as in the case of the caliph, individual rulers must be judged in terms of their acts. 'The acts of him who seizes control over the imām must be examined. If they are in accordance with the ordinances of *religion* and the requirements of *justice* it is permissible that the usurper be confirmed in his position. ...'[131]

A third major political reality can be found in the disintegration of the empire and its falling into the hands of various princes, many of them Shīʿīs, able to maintain virtual independence. Though Māwardī ideally prefers a limited governorship that would exclude collection of taxes and administration of justice, he is forced by the actual political circumstances to a tacit acceptance of a general governorship with radically expanded duties.[132] Examination of these duties shows that they are almost identical with the duties of the caliph. It is then natural that the qualifications for candidates for both offices should be almost identical except that the governor-general need not be a descendant of Quraysh and that he must have experience with the details of war and taxation.

Even though the expanded jurisdiction of the governors was accepted, the fact remained that most of these men had come to power by the sword rather than, as Muslim theory would require, through appointment by the caliph. Either these governors were illegitimate, or Māwardī was faced with the formidable task of explaining away such an irregular situation. He chooses to accept the amīrate (governorship) by seizure which, contracted involuntarily, means 'that an amīr having seized a territory by force is subsequently invested by the caliph governor of the conquered territory ... in such a case, the governor through his conquest takes exclusive charge of government and administration, and the caliph through his investiture effects the execution of the ordinances of religion'. The investiture by the caliph is obligatory if the usurper fulfils the conditions prerequisite for the free investiture of a governor.[133]

It should be clear by now that the above discussion of the caliphate is hardly theoretical. It shows clearly Māwardī's awareness of political realities and his desire to maintain the caliph as a symbol of the unity of the community and, more important, the prevalence of divine Law.

In the absence of political mechanisms to ensure the election of a qualified caliph, it was inevitable that the title of the caliphate should go to whoever disposed, or had the support, of superior military power.[134] But Māwardī's purpose of safeguarding the *sharīʿa* was never lost sight of by Muslim writers[135] – no, not even by the often maligned Ibn Jamāʿa, to whom Professor Gibb mistakenly attributes 'complete divorce of the imāmate from the *sharīʿa*, and the abandonment of the law in favour of secular absolutism'.[136] In fact Ibn Jamāʿa, like many Muslim writers, accepts the fact that rulership is usually based on superior force, and goes on to demand that the powerful ruler should fulfil the requirements of religion and justice.[137] We have already seen that the fulfilment of the requirements of religion and justice was Māwardī's overriding concern.[138] The requirements of religion have been spelled out in detail in the *sharīʿa*. What are the requirements of justice?

5

Extralegal Criterion

Justice

The question 'What is justice?' is at the very heart of normative political thought. It is no surprise that the definition of justice is the starting point of the first systematic work in political philosophy – Plato's *Republic*. Muslims have defined justice in various ways. For example, a younger contemporary of Māwardī, the Muslim philospher al-ʿĀmirī,[139] accepts the Aristotelian definition of justice as equality. But this does not tell us very much when we realize that what is here meant is proportionate equality, or treating equals equally. The crucial question becomes: 'who are equal?'. To answer this question is to spell out the rules and regulations that govern the relationships of rulers and ruled. It is then not surprising that most attempts at defining justice lead to law – to a government based not on arbitrary will but on law.[140] To Māwardī, as to all Muslims, an ideal polity is a polity in accordance with divine Law.

Māwardī agrees with the Socratic philosophers that a just polity can be attained only in a society of just individuals. Justice in the individual is harmony and balance of the soul. Such balance is attained only when reason restrains passion. This cannot be achieved unless the individual receives proper discipline and education, both of which must start at a very early age.[141] Education in its widest sense must be based not only on religion but also on reason dictating certain standards of conduct, and convention requiring modes of behaviour not necessarily deduced by reason but agreed upon by the wise, educated and well bred.

In addition to education, the individual needs a minimum level of economic well-being, for no individual can be just in his behaviour if he lacks the material for his subsistence.[142] The poor must have their share in the goods of the earth 'so that envy is diminished and hatred resulting from destitution is eliminated'.[143] Māwardī is calling not for economic levelling or egality but for eliminating destitution and ensuring subsistence.

Just as justice in the individual is harmony and balance of the various faculties of the soul, justice in the political community is also harmony and balance among the various groups of society, especially rulers and ruled. Harmony and order is the consequence of obedience to law. Therefore, in the Muslim community, just government is government in accordance with divine Law. Divine Law, since it embodies God's wisdom which encompasses the hereafter as well as this world, is naturally superior to human law even as far as worldly matters are concerned. But the historical evolution of the *sharīʿa* as a scholar's law and the limited jurisdiction of judges meant that the *sharīʿa* was not all-inclusive in practice. Government in accordance with the spirit of Islam could not be attained by mere application of the *sharīʿa* within the limited jurisdiction of the *qāḍī*. The need for an additional criterion was met by the ancient concept of *ʿadl* (justice). Although according to some Muslim writers[144] it formally subsumed the *sharī'a*, *ʿadl* more commonly refers to the extra-*sharīʿa* political criterion[145] – witness the fact that a non-Muslim ruler, the Sassanid Kisrā Anūshirwān, was frequently held up as the paragon of justice.[146] It is in this latter and more limited sense that the word 'justice' will be used in our discussion.

Māwardī's definition of justice represents in its broad outlines a prevalent trend in Muslim thought. Just government should be in the interest of the governed. The model Muslim ruler is represented by an idealized picture of the first four caliphs, who 'considered the sole purpose of the caliphate to be the vitalization of religion and the welfare of the Muslims'.[147] The welfare of the Muslims demands the provision of internal and external security, which are a primary function of any government. A just ruler is responsible for the maintenance of public irrigation works in an otherwise laissez-faire economy. The rulers ought not to participate in economic activities, for this would hinder the flock from making a living.[148] The essence of justice, however, is respect of the rights of private property, and by extension, free (i.e. not forced) labour.[149] Of course, Māwardī does not deny the government the right to collect taxes primarily for the support of an army and police, essential for maintenance of peace and security. Ideally, such taxes must be in accordance with the *sharīʿa*. In fact, however, Māwardī accepts the regulations of governmental bureaux as the operative 'law' (*qānūn*) in regard to financial and military administration.[150]

Another important requirement of justice is the scrupulous respect of custom.[151] Even though Muslim scholars, especially in the first two centuries of Islam, incorporated many elements of local custom within the *sharīʿa*, customary practice remained a crucial criterion defining good and evil.[152] We have already seen how Māwardī entrusted the *muḥtasib* with enforcing elements of customary practice,[153] as part of his duty to command people to do good and to desist from evil.

A further and essential meaning of justice as used in traditional

Islam is moderation. Māwardī, like most Muslim writers, accepts a hierarchic conception of society but rejects rigid stratification, be it on the basis of knowledge or wealth or both.

Even though he had Muʿtazilite leanings, Māwardī would not agree with the Muʿtazilite Jāḥiz, who wrote:

> The commoners are a mere instrument of the elite to be exploited in work and used in assailing the enemy and defending the frontiers. The relation of the commoners to the elite is that of the limbs to a human being ... the commoners are merely a shield for defence and a weapon for fighting. They are to the elite as a coat of mail is to the bowman or a hatchet to the carpenter.[154]

Such rigid views were apparently widespread among the upper classes. A ninth-century bureaucrat writes: 'Justice according to the upper classes is that he [the ruler] drive the commoners through servility and humiliation to submit to [their] superiors'.[155] That the commoners had other ideas is attested to by the same author, who wrote: 'Justice according to the flock is that he [the ruler] should make their condition equal to that of the upper classes'.[156]

Māwardī would agree with the above author that both of these conceptions are extreme and therefore unjust, and that between the rich and poor, the strong and weak, war is inevitable unless each side moderates its views. Māwardī's conception of justice as moderation leads him to reject not only rigid stratification but also the extrapolation of the egalitarian principle from the religious sphere to the social and economic order.

What is the relation of Māwardī's views on justice to those of other Muslim writers and to pre-Islamic conceptions? Would the concept of justice embodied in the ancient principles of government be still adequate even after Islam had replaced previous religions? A prevalent trend in Muslim political thought would answer the second question in the affirmative. Ṭurṭūshī, born in the year that Māwardī died, illustrates this trend when he writes: 'Having examined the histories of past communities and bygone kings, ... I could distinguish between two categories: statutes or religion and principles of government'.[157] Ṭurṭūshī, as a Muslim, naturally contests the validity of the religious statutes of the ancients,[158] and holds that only the *sharīʿa* embodies 'divine justice';[159] but he endorses heartily their principles of government[160] as an adequate embodiment of 'conventional justice'.[161] 'No imperial dynasty without an army, no army without taxes, no taxes without prosperity, no prosperity without justice' is a Sassanid maxim that turns up, in slightly varied forms, in most Arabic works on govermnent and administration.[162] The above maxim could imply that the raison d'être of justice is the maintenance of the dynasty, in which case justice would easily become the minimum that the rulers must do in order to preserve their dynastic rule. Māwardī, as a man of religion, would not accept this interpretation. The ultimate end of justice is not the power of the ruler, but the welfare of the community and the fulfilment of God's Law, to which the ruler's power is only a means. This Muslim view is illustrated by Ghazzālī's explicit modification of the above maxim such as to put religion ahead of dynasty.[163]

Another Muslim modification of the Sassanid concept of justice is the recurrent demand that a ruler must be available to hear personally the flock's grievances.[164] The remoteness and pomp of the Sassanid emperor is usually contrasted with the Muslim ideal of accessibility and simplicity[165] – an ideal that clearly harks back to the model of the Arab tribal chief.

Finally, Māwardī, like many a Muslim writer, would disagree with those authors[166] whose Sassanid conception of justice called for rigid stratification of the various classes of society. Māwardī, while accepting hierarchy of rank, would agree with ʿĀmirī's ideal of limited mobility with careers open to talent: 'It is known that the Persian rulers ... forbade their subjects to advance from one rank to another higher one. Such an attitude results in preventing many good qualities from achieving equitable distribution. It incapacitates noble souls and discourages them, so that they do not aspire to high rank.'[167] Needless to say, this is not a call for the modern ideal of equal opportunity, but a plea against closing the doors in the face of an exceptional man who might be of extraordinary ability in spite of a disadvantaged background.

A definition of justice will not be complete without a discussion of the way in which the concept operates in society. How is justice to be achieved? Or, to put the question in the more appropriate negative form, how is prevalent injustice to be corrected?

Traditional Muslim political thought, like medieval western thought, championed a hierarchic conception of society.[168] In such a society, the lower, if it does not fulfil its duties, is naturally corrected by the higher. Just as the responsibility for dealing with a misbehaving child lies with the head of the family, responsibility for remedying the injustices of the bureaucracy lies with the head of the political community.[169] Māwardī is very critical of a disintegrating and oppressive bureaucracy that was overmilking the flock. He recommends fundamental administrative reforms based on his view that the government's raison d'être is not aggrandizement of the bureaucracy but the welfare of the Muslim community.

Māwardī recommends that the size of the bureaucracy should be kept to a minimum, for its cost is a heavy burden on the community,[170] and that bureaucratic posts should not be passed on from father to son without regard to ability.[171] Government officials should respect private property and desist from its forcible seizure.[172] They should not be allowed to make what they could on the job, 'for such practice leads to exploitation of the flock'.[173] Instead they should be paid set salaries in accordance with the stipulations of the official register.[174] They should also have security of tenure,

> for when it is known that the ruler pursues a policy of frequent dismissals and transfers, every official, thinking that his days in office are numbered, would work for today and neglect the morrow, grab the wealth at the beginning of his appointment as a preparation for the time when he is out of office. So when he is dismissed, he leaves the land in disrepair. His successor would act in like manner, aggravating the disorder. Thus it is not long before the land is ruined through the plundering of the tax officials.[175]

Taxes are considered too high, and the practice of farming out the collection of tax revenues to the highest bidder is decried as leading to extortion and oppression.[176] In order to prevent arbitrary levies, the taxes on the flock should be clearly spelled out in the caliph's register.[177]

To restore justice in accordance with the above principles, Māwardī calls for the revival of the office for the redress of wrongs, disposing of the highest authority. The most important function of the holder of this office is to ensure respect by the powerful of the right of private property and to audit tax collection and expenditure to see that they are in accordance with administrative regulations, and to check irregularities and cheating on the part of revenue collectors, financial secretaries and army leaders.[178]

6

Reactions to Injustice

Before Māwardī

It is natural that Māwardī should look to the higher to correct the lower. But what is to be done when the ultimate holders of power, rather than exercising their authority to redress wrongs, do themselves commit injustice? To say that Islam always counselled absolute submission would be a crude oversimplification that misses a society's dynamism reflected in the continuous tension between the ideal and real. By Māwardī's time, this question had puzzled many Muslims and received a variety of answers ranging from absolute submission[179] to revolution and tyrannicide.[180]

In analyzing the reactions of Muslims to injustice, particular emphasis will naturally be placed on Sunnism, the historically prevalent form of Islam. It is important, however, to keep two points in mind. First, Sunnism cannot be discussed in isolation, for it was defined in relation to more specific opposing doctrines, that is, by the positions and attitudes that it rejected. Second, and related to the first point, Sunnism is by no means a uniform body of doctrines, but represents a variety of attitudes within broadly defined limits.

The principal opposition doctrines that defined the limits of what came to be called Sunnī Islam are three: Shīʿism, Khārijism and Muʿtazilism.[181] As we have seen in a preceding section, these sects had their beginnings in the first civil war and expressed varying degrees of opposition to the ascendancy of the Meccan aristocracy. Much of this opposition rallied around ʿAlī, a representative of the new religious leadership – hence the name 'Shīʿa' or 'party [of ʿAlī]'. ʿAlī's willingness to temper force with diplomacy alienated some of his followers, who seceded – hence Khārijites. The Khārijites represented tribal anarchism, resentment against any central authority, and a ready willingness to resort to force in the face of 'injustice'. The Muʿtazila probably had their antecedents in those who adopted a position of neutrality as between ʿAlī and his adversaries.[182]

Those who, on the other hand, accepted the ascendancy of the Meccan aristocracy and the triumph of Muʿāwiya and the Umayyids, are represented by the Murji'a, whose political significance lies in their initial quietism.

The Khārijites' attitude towards the use of force did not undergo appreciable change with the passage of time, and reflected the tribal legitimacy of the raid and the perennial encroachment of the desert on the sown. It is interesting that Khārijism when used as the ideology of independent principalities, usually peripheral, tended to take the more moderate form of the Ibāḍiyya.[183]

While many partisans of ʿAlī (Shīʿīs) rejected the use of force and acquiesced in the Umayyid triumph, ʿAlid legitimism continued to provide a convenient banner of opposition to the Umayyids, and in fact was an important factor in their eventual demise.

The triumphant ʿAbbāsids were faced with the most difficult task of keeping within bounds the revolutionary zeal of extreme Shīʿism. To this end, Muʿtazilite polemics were consciously utilized. However, the eventual failure of extreme Shīʿism, understandable within the context of traditional society, is to be associated not so much with Muʿtazilite polemics as with two important developments: the growth of Twelver Shīʿism and the formation of the Fāṭimid empire.

Twelver Shīʿism that crystallized in the fourth Muslim (tenth Christian) century rallied Shīʿi sentiment to an ethical rather than a political ideal. The psychological significance of the concept of a hidden imām is the affirmation that political reality has fallen short of the Muslim ideal. But rather than preaching fulfilment of the ideal, they saw in unfulfilment an ethical challenge and consoled themselves by the view that it is more virtuous to be good in a polity that is far from ideal.[184] Twelver Shīʿīs thus preached political quietism and postponed political fulfilment until the end of time and the appearance of the hidden imām.

Extreme Shīʿism, under the banner of Fāṭimid Ismāʿīlism, did attempt fulfilment here and now, and in fact succeeded in establishing an empire with universal claims. As often happens with dogmatic revolutionary movements, Ismāʿīlīs in power demanded submission as absolute as the rebellion which they advocated when out of power.[185] The claims of Ismāʿīlīs met with a great deal of resistance from the learned, who had become used to seeing themselves as political inheritors of the Prophet and the true guardians of Muslim ideology.[186]

Extreme Shīʿīs, aware of the use of religion to enforce an unsatisfactory social and political order,[187] did borrow generously from Greek philosophy.[188] But they by no means rejected Islam. Islam continued to provide a set of symbols and a medium of communication for ruler and rebel alike. The natural hostility of the orthodox to political philosophy was increased by the association of philosophy with Shīʿī opposition, that relied not only on propaganda, as in the case of Ikhwān al-Ṣafāʾ, but also on the use of force, as with the Ismāʿīlīs.[189]

Having discussed the Khārijite and Shīʿite opposition, let us now turn to the Muʿtazilites. The political significance of Muʿtazilism is not so much its use under the Umayyids as the ideology of the ʿAbbāsid revolution (Nyberg thesis),[190] as its utilization by the triumphant ʿAbbāsids to combat the revolutionary zeal of extreme Shīʿīs.[191] Like the Shīʿīs, and most political thinkers for that matter, the Muʿtazilites saw justice in the unity of 'truth' with power. But rather than looking for the unity of truth and power in one man who will bring about political fulfilment here and now (extreme Shīʿīs) or in the eschatological future (Twelver Shīʿīs), the Muʿtazilites held that the *'ulamā'*, guardians of the truth, should set up a ruler from among their midst.[192] Their brief success came when they were able to convert or ally themselves with existing rulers, for example Maʾmūn, Muʿtaṣim and Wāthiq (first half of the ninth century) or Buwayhid princes (second half of the tenth century and first half of the eleventh century). The weakness of the Muʿtazilite ideology was its inability to establish adequate links with the populace. This was related to its rationalism and intellectual elitism.[193] The hostility of most Muslim rulers to Muʿtazilism is due not so much to disagreement on strictly theological questions, as to the subversive influence of the Muʿtazila. Not only did they hold it to be their moral duty to command what was good and prohibit what was evil, but they also insisted on their ultimate right of resistance. Although they opposed irresponsible and rash use of force, and counselled taking up arms only when the probability of success was high,[194] they never gave up their right to use organized force to remedy injustice.

It is by no means surprising that the Khārijites, the Muʿtazilites, and some Shīʿītes, insisted that obedience is conditional. In a society that considers God's revelation all-inclusive, no ruler can demand absolute obedience unless he could claim to be the sole guardian of God's revelation. Only Ismāʿīlī rulers made such a claim. In contrast, the majority of Muslims accepted the body of the learned as the true guardians of religious ideology.

Government on the imperial level had little room for political participation, and to maintain its authority attempted to limit interference by those outside the government. We have already seen how the *ʿulamā'*'s success in asserting their claim to the guardianship of the *sharīʿa* was at the price of excluding many governmental matters not only from the operative *sharīʿa*, i.e. the *qāḍī*'s jurisdiction, but also from theoretical formulations. That the formulated *sharīʿa* failed to incorporate the concept of political justice is clearly illustrated by the admission of Muslims that a ruler might follow the *sharīʿa* and still be oppressive.[195] We have also seen how the people were denied the right to judge politics by such writers as Ibn al-Muqaffaʿ, who limited the applicability of the tradition 'No obedience is due to any creature in disobeying the Creator' to strictly religious matters.

Granted that the *'ulamā'* and the common people should be disqualified from appraising and, as a possible consequence, opposing most of the ruler's actions, on the ground that politics is a specialized art, how about that segment of the intellectual elite that is skilled in the political art – namely, members of the bureaucracy?

Ibn al-Muqaffa''s hierarchic view of government and society leads him to reject any opposition to the ruler's policies even by the bureaucracy:

> if you have the misfortune to be associated with a ruler who does not desire the well-being of his flock, you are faced with two choices that are equally bad. Either you side with the ruler against the flock, which would be the ruin of religion, or you side with the flock against the ruler, which would be the ruin of the world. You have no way out except death or flight.[196]

The tenth-century philosopher Fārābī agreed with Ibn al-Muqaffa' that he who is qualified to judge the acts of a ruler has, when faced with injustice, only two options: death or flight. But Fārābī was less optimistic about the existence of just polities to which the virtuous might flee: 'a virtuous man is prohibited from staying in an iniquitous polity and is obligated to migrate to virtuous polities if such actually exist at his time. But if they are non-existent, the virtuous man would be a stranger in the world, his life abominable, and death better for him than life.'[197]

A contemporary of Māwardī, the historian-philosopher-bureaucrat Miskawayh, met the above dilemma by accepting imperfection as natural to all outward concerns and suggesting that the only true kingdom is the kingdom within.[198] Miskawayh's attitude might be sound psychological advice, especially in a milieu where the individual had little expectation of controlling the external world. Yet concern with the inner kingdom, while politically relevant, is no substitute for polities. The concern of politics goes beyond the achievement of balance within the individual to the attainment of harmony in the community. It is true that the involvement of the individual in the central government of an empire could not be as crucial or absorbing as his participation in the government of a polis. Still, for many Muslims, the problems of imperial government were of definite concern.

The Muslim ideal is that government should be in the interest of the governed. Therefore, to many Muslims, the individual's obedience to the rulers was always conditional not only on execution of the divine Law but also on some extralegal criterion as justice or public interest.[199] However the individual might define justice or public interest, the question that concerns us here is what is to be done if the ruler falls short of the ideal.

By Māwardī's time, many Sunnīs agreed with Khārijites, Muʿtazilites and Shīʿīs that an unjust or sinful ruler must be deposed.[200] In the absence of political institutions, force was the usual means for the deposition of unjust rulers. The frequent resort to violence in the first centuries of Islam led a large number of *ʿulamā'* to adopt quietism. In discussing the Shīʿīs, we have already had occasion to refer to the quietist position of the Twelvers. Among the Sunnīs, the quietist movement was spearheaded by the Traditionalists. All sorts of arguments were marshalled to oppose the use of force against the rulers. These arguments emphasized the need for unity and the importance of ethical rather than political responsibility. The emphasis on unity is understandable given the difficulty of maintaining an extensive political community. The de-emphasis of political responsibility found its Qur'ānic justification in the following verse: '0 ye who believe, let your concern be yourselves. He who goes astray will do ye no harm as long as ye are rightly guided.'[201] The specific application of this attitude to unjust rulers found expression in a tradition attributed to the Prophet in which he counsels: 'Listen and obey [unjust rulers], for their responsibility is to fulfil only their duties and your responsibility is to fulfil only your duties'.[202] Of those who recommended inaction in the face of injustice, there were some who argued that action might involve injuring others and that it would be nobler to suffer than inflict suffering.[203] Unjust rulers are to be accepted, according to other traditions, because God in His wisdom intended them as a punishment: 'For they are only a punishment that God inflicts on whomsoever He wills. Do not receive the punishment of God with anger and indignation, but receive it with humility and resignation.'[204]

It is psychologically difficult to hold that injustice can go unpunished. Rectification of injustice was therefore left to God, who alone was to inflict punishment and to grant reward. Man may pray to God, who is especially responsive to the plight of the oppressed.[205] If punishment did not befall the unjust ruler in this life, then it would surely do so in the hereafter. True justice would be achieved not by the persistent effort of men but by a cataclysmic act, the coming of the Messiah who will fill the earth with justice as it is now filled with injustice.

These rationalizations and psychological compensations did not disguise the tension between the ideal and the real. The very preface of the above-quoted tradition counselling obedience to unjust rulers illustrates clearly and dramatically the Muslim's awareness of the divergence of this counsel from the Muslim ideal. Muhammad is asked: 'O Prophet of God, if rulers come to power over us who demand what is their due and withhold that which is our due, what would you command us?'[206] The Prophet turns his back to the questioner. The question is posed again. The Prophet again evades it. But the questioner persists and asks a third time. Even then, the Prophet has to be pulled by the shoulder by one of his companions before he would give his reluctant answer demanding obedience.

Beyond the above justifications of obedience, the Traditionalists attempted to move closer to the ideal by emphasizing the importance of free speech including free criticism of rulers not only by the learned but also by any commoner who might be knowledgeable and capable.[207] Professing the truth to an unjust ruler was considered of such importance that it was usually recommended to the individual Muslim even though it might entail danger to his life and limb. It is significant that under such circumstances the only other act that was similarly recommended was the defence of the faith against disbelief.[208]

7

Reactions to Injustice

Māwardī

The preceding responses to injustice were part of the psychological and intellectual inheritance of Māwardī's age. We have seen how Māwardī naturally looked to the higher in the hierarchy of power to redress the injustice of the lower. But what is to be done if the highest power itself is unjust?

That the highest power was in fact unjust is made abundantly clear by Māwardī. For example, he admonishes the ruler to respect the right of the flock and not to compete with it in various economic activities. 'Sometimes the ruler begrudges them [the flock] their gain and interferes and shares in it by engaging in trade along with the merchants or in agriculture along with the farmers. This is a violation of the rules of administration and the conditions of leadership.'[209] In support of this injunction, Māwardī quotes the prophetic tradition: 'when the ruler takes the trade, the flock is neglected'.

That the flock was indeed neglected Māwardī indicates by repeating an anecdote in which the founder of the 'Abbāsid dynasty is addressed by one of his flock, a stranger, in the following words: 'You then sent your tax officials, reinforced by men, weapons and beasts to levy and collect taxes ... neglecting the wronged and troubled, the hungry and naked, the weak and poor, when there is not a single one of these but has a rightful claim to some of these revenues'.[210]

Māwardī argues that such injustice and neglect of the flock was true of most rulers after the first four caliphs: the Rashidūn 'were succeeded by those who desired this world ... and put it first; lived in luxury; utilized the wealth of God and his servants as a means of their own power and dominance; and neglected the flock'.[211]

When faced with injustice of worldly power, the medieval mind often resorted to exhortation so that power might reform itself, or looked for redress to the yet higher power of God. By the eleventh century, the realities of power in the Muslim world had changed in such a way as to permit Māwardī a novel response. The imperial structure of western Asia which survived in Islam under the guise of the caliphate, suffered its final collapse in the middle of the tenth century at the hands of the Buwayhids. The caliph, theoretically the religious and political leader of the community, lost most of his power. The actual separation of religious and political leadership was described by a contemporary of Māwardī in the following words:

> According to them [the astrologers], dominion and kingship have passed during the last days of Muttaqī and the beginnings of the reign of Mustakfī from the ʿAbbāsids to the Buwayhids. What remains in the hands of the ʿAbbāsid caliph is power only in matters of religion and faith but not in royal and worldly affairs, just as the Jewish roshgaluth has only religious leadership to the exclusion of kingship and dominion.[212]

Māwardī's response to the changing circumstances is on two levels. On the first level, he reaffirms his allegiance to the Muslim ideal of the caliph as the religious and political leader of the community. On the second level, he attempts to salvage what he could from the then existing situation. He was convinced that political power was not merely organized force but needed also ideological legitimatization. It was his aim to safeguard the caliphate as the nominal head of the political community and the actual head of the religious institution, and to use the caliph's legitimizing power to influence princes to act in accordance with religion and justice. This position is still compatible with a descending view of polity and society, for the caliph, though weaker than various princes, still disposes of a theoretically higher authority.

Thus Māwardī deals with the princes who seize control over the imām (i.e. Buwayhids) in the following manner: 'if the usurper's acts do not conform to the ordinances of *religion* and *justice*, then he may not be confirmed and it is necessary that the caliph seek the assistance of those who will restrain the usurper's hand and put an end to his domination'.[213] According to some chroniclers, this is in fact what happened three years before Māwardī's death when, on the invitation of the caliph,[214] the Sunnī Saljūq Sultan Tughril, who had previously received Māwardī as the caliph's emissary, entered Baghdad and initiated a new dynasty.

Similarly, in dealing with princes who usurped control of outer provinces, Māwardī made legitimization by the caliph dependent on the princes' 'observance of the stipulations of divine Law and the guarding of the religious statutes'. The stipulations of the divine Law that are thus safeguarded are:

1. Maintenance of the office of the imām as the vicegerent of the Prophet and the administrator of the affairs of religion, so that the requirements of the Law for setting up the imāma will be fulfilled and the rights and duties deriving therefrom will be safeguarded.
2. Manifestation of religious obedience through which the legal

state of rebellion is terminated and the sin of insubordination is abrogated.

3. Agreement on mutual friendship and assistance so that the Muslims will be powerful vis à vis non-Muslims.
4. Validation of the contract pertaining to the delegation of religious functions, and the judgments and decisions deriving therefrom.
5. Legalization of the collection of taxes stipulated by Law, so that the taxpayer would be fulfilling his religious duty and the tax-collector would be taking what is legally permitted.
6. Regular application of legal penalties, for the person of the believer is inviolable and his freedom limited only by God's Law.
7. Provision for the community, in upholding religion, of a power which would restrain people from committing acts prohibited by God – a power that the obedient are commanded [by the caliph] to accept as lawful and the recalcitrant are summoned to obey.[215]

To date, the only serious study of Māwardī is that of Professor Gibb.[216] Professor Gibb's conclusion about the amīrate by seizure, reiterated in his later articles,[217] presents us with a serious problem and deserves to be quoted at length. In referring to the legal conditions enumerated above, he writes:

> If these conditions are fulfilled al-Māwardī goes so far as to say that the caliph must grant the conqueror this recognition and authorization, in order to forestall the danger of driving him into rebellion; and even if they are not fulfilled the caliph may do so in order to induce him to make submission, though in the latter case he should also appoint a representative as a valid executive authority.

Professor Gibb does not make clear the jurisdiction of this executive or his relation to the usurper. Gibb goes on to say:

> But what were the legal principles upon which the validity of such sweeping concessions could be based? ... It must be supposed that in his zeal to find some arguments by which at least the show of legality could be maintained, al-Māwardī did not realize that he had undermined the foundations of all law. Necessity and expedience may indeed be respectable principles, but only when they are not invoked to justify disregard of the law. It is true that he seeks to limit them to this one case, but to admit them at all was the thin edge of the wedge. Already the whole structure of the juristic theory of the caliphate was beginning to

crumble, and it was not long before the continued application of these principles brought it crashing to the ground.[218]

'Sweeping concession', 'undermining the foundations of all law', and 'disregard of the law' are phrases that can hardly be applied to Māwardī's formulation. Professor Gibb's dramatic and negative verdict is based on a misunderstanding of the text. Māwardī definitely does not permit legitimization of a usurper who does not fulfil the legal conditions enumerated above. The conditions that Māwardī was referring to are those necessary for the free appointment of the governor – principally the qualifications of probity and knowledge of the Law that would enable him to give independent judgment.

If the usurper lacks the necessary probity and legal knowledge, he may be confirmed in his office, but only if he accepts a qualified representative of the caliph. The relation of the Caliph's representative to the usurper is made very clear by Māwardī, who leaves financial and military matters to the usurper but considers the caliph's representative as the sole valid executor of religious and legal affairs.

Thus we see that Māwardī hardly disregarded the Law. On the contrary, his main concern was its proper execution. But does Māwardī's statement that 'the usurping governor through his conquest takes exclusive charge of government and administration' mean that conquest legitimizes the governor's powers in these areas? To answer this question, we must turn to *Tashīl al-naẓar*, where Māwardī deals with the strictly political aspects of usurpation. He asserts that a rule based on force becomes legitimate only if the ruler is just with his flock. While appointment by the caliphs is indispensable for delegating authority in the religious sphere, Māwardī implies that the just conduct of a usurper towards his flock is tantamount to his receiving delegated authority in the non-religious sphere, for he calls just rule of a usurper rule by delegation.[219]

The effect of Māwardī's prescription is to leave to the inferior power of the caliphate the right to influence the superior power of worldly princes. The caliph's, influence was based on two important facts. In the first place, long after the decline of his power, the caliph remained in the eyes of the masses the supreme legitimate leader of the Muslim community. In the second place, he was the symbolic head of a large group of *'ulamā'* who had an important influence in society, and, as judges, in the bureaucracy.

Māwardī emphasized the importance of a harmonious relation between caliph and *'ulamā'*. When the unjust caliph, in the anecdote quoted above, cries out on hearing of the torture that awaits him on the Day of Judgment, 'What recourse have I?', the stranger is made to answer: 'People have distinguished men who are sought after in matters of religion; make them your retinue and consult them in your affairs; they will guide you to the right way'. When the caliph complains that he had tried to cooperate with the learned but they had shunned him, the stranger retorts: 'They fear that you will have them behave as you have. But if you will open your doors and make yourself accessible, support the wronged and restrain the wrongdoers, collect religious taxes lawfully and divide them equitably, I guarantee that they will come and help you to achieve the well-being of the community.'[220]

As for the learned both in and outside the bureaucracy, they also left much to be desired. While frankly pointing out their faults, Māwardī attempts to give reasons for their misconduct and to recommend remedial measures. He admits that 'contrary to what ought to have been, lust for worldly goods has become, especially in our time, the custom of the learned'.[221] In another place, he attempts to explain their lust by suggesting 'perhaps the lack of material possessions and the weakness of circumstance has induced some of them to laxity, dishonourable conduct and dubious behaviour'.[222] Māwardī's recommendation for correcting the behaviour of the learned who worked in the bureaucracy as judges is that they should be paid well 'so that they will shun avarice for the flock's wealth'.[223]

The caliph, in cooperation with the *'ulamā'*, guardians of the religious ideology, has the responsibility to restrain unjust rulers through granting or withholding legitimization. But what about the average Muslim? When relative justice prevails, Māwardī advises the individual Muslim to conform and accept his situation in life. 'Be devoted to your affairs, content with your fortune, at peace with your neighbours; conform to the customs of your times, accept the leadership of those above you, be sympathetic to those below you; ...'.[224]

The individual Muslim, however, is not obligated to obey a ruler who does not fulfil the requirements of religion and justice. Māwardī warns that resistance is an anticipated consequence of injustice. When the ruler does not fulfil his duties, 'his flock will harbour disobedience and hatred against him; and to proclaim these, they will await opportunities and lie in expectation of a change in his fortune'.[225]

Furthermore, the individual has the positive moral duty to command good and prohibit evil. This is the closest that Māwardī and Islam come to the concept of civic responsibility. If the evildoer is an organized group, for example, government, Māwardī holds that forbidding evil is obligatory if the individual has supporters and can be effective, otherwise he must desist from rash acts. Māwardī, like Muslims in general, does not think of devising political mechanisms or organizations to aggregate individual Muslims for effective resistance. Instead he depends on existing centres of power, usually based on tribal or slave armies, and hopes to effect change through the informal process of withholding or bestowing religious legitimization.

8

Reactions to Injustice

After Māwardī

What were the prevalent intellectual attitudes towards injustice after Māwardī? Religious attitudes toward unjust rulers are closely linked with the relation of men of religion to the rulers in general, or, to put it more abstractly, of *sharī'a* to *siyāsa*.[226]

The view that *sharī'a* covered all aspects of life including politics remained the ideal of most Muslims. For example, Subkī (d. 1370) writes: 'The interest of God's creatures is in obedience to the Law of the Creator who knows best what is good and bad for them. The revealed Law of our Prophet Muḥammad, may God's prayers and peace be upon him, guarantees all man's interests in this life and the next. Corruption results only through deviation from the revealed Law.'[227]

The tension between this ideal and political reality is at the heart of all Muslim political thought. In fact, government fell largely outside the province of the *sharī'a* as administered by Muslim judges. Extra *sharī'a* administration was known as *siyāsa*, the ideals of which were embodied in the concept of justice. That the *sharī'a* was by no means all-inclusive is illustrated dramatically by Subkī's older contemporary, Taftāzānī, who, in a famous work on theology, states that a ruler may follow the *sharī'a* and still be unjust.[228] Subkī's insistence that the only law is divine Law and that one may not speak of administrative 'law' but only of 'ways' or 'practice' is the prevalent Muslim position.[229] But his statement that '*Siyāsa* is utterly useless, nay even harmful to country and flock, and leads inevitably to disorder and chaos'[230] merely dramatizes the tension between the ideal and the real without attempting a resolution.

Like Māwardī, the greatest Muslim thinkers warned against both the futile insistence on absolute realization of the Muslim ideal and the wholesale acceptance of Muslim reality. For example, the famous Ibn Taymiyya (d. 1328) criticized on the one hand those who would use force to realize their interpretation of the ideal Muslim polity, and on the other those who would disregard government in the belief that the demands of politics are incompatible with divine Law. The first position would lead to bloodshed and chaos; the second would leave politics to those who see in government an opportunity for the aggrandizement of the rulers at the expense of the flock. Ibn Taymiyya's prescription is for a moderate solution – a compromise that accepts the difficulties of fulfilling the Muslim ideal and yet does not neglect government, but attempts to salvage what is possible through involvement in 'the art of the possible'. This is what Ibn Taymiyya calls *siyāsa sharʿiyya*, or government in accordance with divine Law.[231] Such a government would accept the realities of power that accrue to wealth and status, and would aim at realizing not the good but the lesser evil. In judging such a government of compromise, the ethical criterion of intentions assumes added importance.

Another famous writer who, like Māwardī, attempted to relate *sharīʿa* to *siyāsa* was Ibn Qayyim al Jawziyya (d. 1356), who was a Ḥanbalite contemporary of Subkī. Ibn Qayyim agreed completely with Ibn ʿAqīl (d. 1119) who, starting with the Muslim ideal, as expressed by Shāfiʿī, that 'no *siyāsa* is valid unless it accords with the *sharʿ*', goes on to say: 'If you mean by your statement "accords with the *sharʿ*" that it does not contradict what the *sharʿ* specifically stipulates, that would be correct; but if you mean that no *siyāsa* is valid unless it is specifically stipulated in the *sharʿ*, that would be an error and an imputation of error to the companions of the Prophet.'[232] Ibn ʿAqīl, like Māwardī, believed that while the spirit of the *sharīʿa* must be all pervasive, its actual formulations were not all inclusive. The *sharīʿa* may not be contradicted but it may definitely be supplemented. Ibn ʿAqīl thus defines *siyāsa* as 'that which actually draws people towards well-being and away from corruption, even though it might be neither laid down by the messenger nor revealed by God'.[233]

Like Māwardī and Ibn Taymiyya, Ibn Qayyim, critical of all those whose narrow conception of the *sharīʿa* would lead to its divorce from government,[234] attempts to give the political concept of justice the sanction of divine Law.

> God, may He be praised, has made clear in the laws which He revealed that His aim is the establishment of justice among His worshippers and the fulfilment of equity by men. Any way that leads to justice and equity is part of and not contrary to religion. Therefore it may not be said that just *siyāsa* is incompatible with the stipulation of the *sharʿ*. On the contrary, just *siyāsa* is in harmony with the content of the *sharʿ* – nay, an integral part of it. Following your idiomatic usage we use the word '*siyāsa*' which is in fact nothing but the justice of God and His messenger.[235]

Māwardī's prescription in the absence of institutionalization did not resolve the increasing tension between *sharīʿa* and *siyāsa*. In fact, by Mamlūk times, the word *siyāsa'*, in addition to its general meaning as administration outside the *qāḍī*'s jurisdiction, assumed an additional and more specific technical meaning. Thus a fourteenth-century manual defines *siyāsa'* as inflicting, for a criminal offence, punishment harsher than stipulated in the *shar'*, in order to ensure order.

Such practice is dealt with in a manuscript on *siyāsa' shar'iyya* by Basnawī (d. 1567). Basically, he agrees with Māwardī, who is quoted at great length, that government should not be divorced from the *sharī'a*. But while Māwardī insists that all government officials, although they might have greater leeway in investigating a criminal offence, are strictly bound by the Law in the determination of penalties, Basnawī allows the ruler to exceed these penalties. In defence of his position, Basnawī marshals many legal principles that allow for leniency and take extenuating circumstances into account. Two themes recur in Basnawī's rationalization. First, changing times call for changing legal ordinances. Times of trouble demand harsher penalties for criminal offences. Second, in a period of disorder, concern for public interest makes it legally permissible, indeed obligatory, to inflict individual harm in order to avoid public injury.[236]

In spite of Basnawī's extreme concessions, Māwardī's insistence that *siyāsa* is a necessary supplement to the *sharī'a*, and must not contradict it but must be in harmony with its spirit (i.e. just), is the starting point for many Muslim political thinkers including such modernists as Khayr al-Dīn[237] (d. 1890) and Rashīd Riḍā[238] (d. 1935).

That the spirit of the *sharī'a* must pervade all aspects of life including politics is an ideal that no Muslim could challenge. But the extrapolation of this position into the claim that the *'ulamā'*, as guardian of the *sharī'a*, have the right to concern themselves with politics produced sharp differences among the *'ulamā'*.

Two tendencies can be distinguished. On the one hand, there were those who, satisfied with their rarely contested right to be the sole guardians of the *sharī'a*, would give the ruler a free hand in *siyāsa*. On the other hand, there were those, larger in number, who, like Māwardī, insisted on their right to concern themselves with the behaviour of the rulers and to sit in judgment even on their very right to rule.

Examination of sixteen printed works[239] ranging between the tenth and the twentieth centuries, revealed that the overwhelming majority of writers in interpreting the verse 'Obey those in command over you'[240] refused to restrict references to the ruler, and insisted on including the *'ulamā'* especially if the ruler did not meet *shar'ī* standards.

Thus the early nineteenth-century Ottoman author of *The Salvation of the Flock is in Obedience to the Imām* illustrates the minority position when he insists that those in command are only the rulers, and that the *'ulamā'* may not interfere in worldly matters but must obey just like any other Muslim. The author's very words show that many *'ulamā'* did not accept such a limitation of their role:

> The Ottoman dynasty ... favoured the *'ulamā'* of its times by raising their status, esteemed them and increased their influence by delivering into their hands the reins of its affairs; and honoured them and treated them better than *'ulamā'* had been treated in the past by most caliphs – all of this out of respect for them and in deference to their learning. But they, being conceited, proved themselves unworthy of this honour. They did not realize that such attention was given to them as a special favour but thought that they deserved it as of right, so they resorted to preposterous and fantastic claims – to the point that they had the audacity to oppose the imām of the time, and the impudence to deny that the present ruler, their benefactor, was the rightful imām and caliph ...[241]

Throughout Islamic history, most 'ulamā' rejected the position of the above author and agreed with Māwardī that they had the right and duty to talk to the ruler and to influence him to fulfil the requirements of religion and justice.[242]

After Māwardī's time, the Muslim concept of the ideal ruler did not undergo any appreciable change. Similarly, reactions to injustice did not differ from those of the early Muslim centuries. What did change was the distribution of the various trends, and the strength of differing tendencies. The problem of the proper response to religious and political injustice continued to perplex Muslims.[243] There were still those who advised as a last resort migration to just polities.[244] But the conditions and attitudes that produced injustice in one principality were more likely than not to produce injustice in another. Migration could resolve the dilemma of a few individuals but not of the political community as a whole. Some intellectuals, while agreeing with the Greeks that the self-sufficient man was either a beast or a demi-god, still advocated as an extraordinary measure individualism and withdrawal from the community.[245] The weakness of this position, even as an alternative for the few, is that it optimistically assumes injustice to be the exception rather than the rule.

Most Muslim thinkers continued to hold that ideally an unjust ruler must be removed. Sunnīs could not easily discard this principle, for it was their retort to the Shī'ī claim of the necessity for an infallible imām.[246] But how is an unjust ruler to be removed? Khārijite views on resistance, reflecting tribal challenge of settled life, never attained prominence among Muslim thinkers who represented settled communities in general and urban centres in particular. Extreme Shī'ism was doomed to a peripheral existence, and was discredited by the Fāṭimid experience and the Ismāʿīlī demand for absolute submission. Even Muʿtazilism, which advocated discreet use of force, suffered a decline with the advent of the Saljūqs and received its death-blow with the Mongol invasion.

The Muʿtazilite position advocating responsible and restrained use of organized force – essentially Māwardī's position – was championed by Māwardī's contemporary, the famous Ibn Ḥazm (d. 1058).[247] A generation after Māwardī, al-Juwaynī (d. 1085) stated the right of resistance in no uncertain terms.[248] But Juwaynī's student, the great al Ghazzālī (d. 1111), formulated the position that was destined to gather increasing support among the *ʿulamā'* in the following centuries. He conceded the right of free criticism but insisted that only the ruler had the right to use force.[249]

The Qur'ānic injunction to prohibit evil, which implied to Māwardī and the Muʿtazila individual responsibility and ultimately the right to use force, was usually explained away in later times by limiting the definition of evil to disbelief, by restricting the means of prohibition to verbal criticism to the exclusion of the use of force, and by claiming that this responsibility is communal and not individual.[250]

The fourteenth-century Abū Ḥayyān (d. 1345) stands out as a voice in the wilderness when he insists that prohibiting evil is a duty incumbent upon all individuals in the community; that evil is not only disbelief but refers to any infraction of the divine Law; and that the means of prohibition cannot exclude the use of force.[251]

Since the thirteenth century, the most popular theological works either declared that between injustice and rebellion Muslims must choose the lesser evil,[252] or went a step further and argued that injustice is always the lesser evil when compared with rebellion and sedition.[253]

In effect, Māwardī's vision of the caliph realizing the ideals of religion and justice by selectively bestowing or withholding legitimization remained a mere vision. It made some sense in late Buwayhid times, when the caliph not only maintained his religious leadership of the *ʿulamā'* but was surrounded by a number of weak princes competing for legitimization, and had a limited influence on the Sunnī population and the Sunnī Turkish mercenaries in the service of the Shīʿī princes. But from the middle of the eleventh century, a number of important developments militated against Māwardī's vision.

First, the caliph's influence vis-à-vis the strong Sunnī Saljūqs of the second half of the eleventh century was much less than his influence vis-à-vis the weak Shīʿī princes of the first half of the same century. It is true that the caliph's position was temporarily enhanced during the decline of Saljūq power, but with the coming of the Mongols (in the thirteenth century) the caliphate, transferred to Mamlūk Egypt, sank lower than ever, and, after the Ottoman conquest of Egypt (in the sixteenth century), no longer had a separate representative, but was claimed by the Ottoman ruler.

Second, after Māwardī's death, and with the coming of the Saljūqs, the rulers assumed greater control over the *'ulamā'* through the institutionalization of religious education[254] and regularization of subsidies and patronage.

Third, beginning in the twelfth century, the Muslim world witnessed a rapid growth of Ṣūfism, which, like Twelver Shī'ism and Sunnī Traditionalism, tended towards quietism. Ṣūfism emphasized the spiritual over the worldly, and channelled Muslim fighting energies towards expanding the community rather than reforming it. For example, the Ottoman dynasty, which at last succeeded in conquering the heart of the Byzantine empire (1452), had its beginning in a Ṣūfī *ghāzī*[255] state. The Ṣūfīs tended to deprecate man's ability to comprehend rationally, let alone judge, the acts of the ruler whom they sanctioned as the axis (*quṭb*) of the world and as chosen by God. For example, Naqshabandī, writing in the late nineteenth century, supported the rulers' position by addressing the following advice and reprimand to Muslims who still insisted on their right to judge the acts of the ruler:

> Beware of opposing them [the rulers] ... if some of their affairs seem utterly incomprehensible to you seek a possible explanation and leave such matters to those in charge. You cannot understand the intentions and the aims of the king because you are not informed of the facts and the essential nature of matters. Your criticism in such cases would be a sign of your ignorance and stupidity; for God, may He be praised and exalted, who is more knowing of His creatures and more concerned for them, and who is more merciful than a mother to her child, has selected the ruler to take charge of His religion and His servants, and, out of His favour delegated to him the reins of power ... Who are you then, O miserable creatures, and what value do your false and vain opinions have, that you should criticize those in command, find fault in their performance, consider their decisions inadequate, and oppose their actions? Beware and beware of indulging in such criticism! God has mercy [only] on him who knows his place and does not exceed his rank. All the above matters are none of your business. The Messenger of God, may God's prayers and peace be upon him, has said, 'a good Muslim does not interfere with that which does not concern him'.[256]

The *'ulamā'*, without an independent organization or a caliph as a focus of leadership, were not very effective as a restraint on unjust rulers. It was not until the nineteenth century that some Muslims through contact with the West became aware for the need of institutionalizing restraint.[257] Two traditional intellectual attitudes incompatible with institutionalized restraint survive into our own age. First, the descending view of society refuses any control of the higher by the lower. The lower may be consulted but the higher has the last word.[258] Second, since the *sharī'a*, or the Qur'ān and Sunna are ideally the law of the Muslim polity, only the *'ulamā'*, those who know religion and divine Law, are considered competent to judge and possibly restrain the rulers.[259] Such a view neglects the element of power which accrues in large measure to those with wealth and position in society.

Present-day Muslims, in attempting to modernize their societies, depend greatly on the ideologies of the dominant West, but find it necessary to continue to use Islamic symbolism. Three important factors help explain why present-day Muslims evince greater attachment to traditional symbolism than had Christians in the early stages of the modern age in the West. First, Islam has always claimed to cover all aspects of life including politics, and therefore Islamic symbolism could not be easily dislodged from political rhetoric. Second, Muslims, faced with a challenging and powerful Christian world, hesitate to reject Muslim symbolism that is an important component of their threatened identity. Third, in an era of mass mobilization, even secular rulers find it useful to employ Islamic symbolism in order to appeal to the masses, whose identity even in the age of nationalism is still basically Islamic.

9

Conclusion

Islamic and Western Political Thought

Māwardī is not a metaphysician but a jurist-theologian whose significance lies more in reflecting important problems and trends in the Muslim political tradition than in his philosophical originality. All through our discussion, we have tried to comprehend this tradition by focusing on Māwardī. In conclusion, it would be useful to attempt a brief comparison of this tradition with the heritage of Western political thought.

Since political thought does not only influence but is also influenced by political institutions, it is more fruitful to compare the imperial Muslim tradition with the empire of the medieval West, rather than with the polls of classical antiquity or the nation-state of modern Europe. Naturally this brief comparison would have to be on a high level of generalization.

Both Islam and Christendom adhered to the ideal of a universal community based on faith in a revealed religion which has its roots in the Judaic tradition of prophecy. The complement of the ideal of universalism was the actuality of localism and political atomization. In both societies, men of religion other than the rulers claimed guardianship of the faith and held that religion provided a pervasive ethical criterion and served as a legitimizer of the rulers.

Both civilizations were pessimistic about the possibilities of attaining perfection in this world and postponed complete fulfilment until the hereafter. In this life, politics could not aspire to attaining the supreme good but had to be satisfied with realizing the lesser evil. It is no surprise then that to the medieval mind the essence of justice was moderation. Both Islam and Christendom had a hierarchic conception of society emphasizing the community over the individual, authority of custom and religion over individual reason, perpetuation of tradition over change and innovation, duties over rights, the good over the true.

Given the fact of strife and instability, both societies stressed the need for harmony and believed that the most united government (i.e. one ruler) can best produce unity. The analogies used to describe the relation of the ruler to the ruled are most instructive. The ruler is like God in His universe, like the patriarchal head of the family, the soul or reason in a body, a shepherd to the flock, or a doctor vis-à-vis his patients. All these analogies emphasize on the one hand the ruler's great authority and on the other his grave responsibility. The ruler is to consult his associates, but he has the last word. The flock is a trust in the hand of the ruler. He is to take into account not their wishes but their interests. His function is limited to providing internal and external security, respecting custom and protecting religion.

In both societies, political thought tended to be deductive rather than empirical[260] and produced principles rather than systematic and elaborate theories.[261] Both Islam and Christendom had an ethical view of politics that depended on the goodness of individuals and neglected political engineering. For example, the ruler is ideally bound by the religious ideology and cannot be arbitrary or demand absolute obedience from the flock. But in the absence of formalized procedures and mechanisms for expressing resistance, the flock was usually counselled to be patient and obey. Since all power is from God, an oppressive ruler might be an intended punishment, and the proper response of the flock is to desist from sin. If people desist from sin and yet injustice prevails, they are to rest assured that God, who is responsive to the flock's prayers, will see to it that injustice would not pay. If injustice seems to pay in this world, the flock is to be consoled by knowing that it will not pay in the hereafter.

In spite of the above similarities, political thought in traditional Islam and medieval Christendom exhibited important differences. Christianity, born in a hostile Roman empire, was forced to produce the nucleus of an organization that had to make a clear distinction between religion and politics, God and Caesar – a distinction that survived into the medieval West in the theory of the two swords, temporal and spiritual. Islam, on the other hand, soon after its birth, served as the banner of an expansive empire. In the absence of an independent religious organization, the distinction between religion and politics was blurred.

The medieval age in the West was ushered in by the Barbarian invasions that destroyed the political fabric of the Christianized Roman empire, but embraced the Christian faith. From this chaos, the church emerged with increasing organization and power that continued into the age of feudalism. The Arabs also engulfed parts of the Christianized Roman empire as well as the Sassanid empire; but they did not adopt the faith of the conquered territories. Rather than destroying the imperial political system, the Arabs, united by the moral force of Islam, perpetuated the imperial tradition of western Asia.

Islam insisted on the ideal that the divine Law applied to all aspects of life including politics, and that the true guardians of divine Law were the men of religion rather than the rulers. If these two principles are carried to their logical conclusion, it could easily follow that the men of religion must be the rulers. In fact, while accepting the above principles as an ideal, the rulers and men of religion worked out an implicit compromise that gave the rulers great leeway in governing their dominion, and largely excluded the functioning of government from the formulated divine Law. The rules and procedures that were the basis of government, having fallen in the province of rulers and their private secretaries rather than men of religion, were never dignified by the name 'law'. The fact that such an arrangement was not made explicit and Muslim ideologues were hesitant to admit the existence or legitimacy of administrative regulations, let alone Roman or natural law, meant that non-*Sharʿī* 'laws' were neither elaborated nor brought into harmony with the religious ideal.

In Christianity, the high Middle Ages witnessed significant changes that increased the contrast between the world of Christendom and that of Islam and prepared the way for the modern age in western Europe. Illustrative of the new spirit of the high Middle Ages was the Thomist synthesis of classical reason and medieval revelation – a synthesis which was destined, after initial resistance, to prevail in the Catholic church. Islamic thinkers insisted on the existence of only one law, divine Law. Aquinas, while relating all law to the eternal law of God, made room for natural law, which is the participation of rational creatures in the eternal law, and human law, which is a specific deduction from natural law. This distinction between human law and divine or natural law meant that ethical injunctions, contrary to the case in Islam, were clearly distinguished from enforceable laws. Thus Aquinas could define human law as an act of will promulgated by him who has coercive power.

Other important developments in the high Middle Ages were the growth of ideas and practices of political consent and participation, elections, corporations, and representative assemblies. More important than these ideas, some of which had their counterpart in Islam, was the embodiment of these ideas in political institutions. A very important factor leading to these developments was the weakness of the central bureaucracies in western Europe as contrasted with the continuous survival of the bureaucratic tradition in Islam.

While in Western Christendom the introduction of classical political philosophy was associated with a process that eventually transformed the medieval order of society far beyond Aquinas's vision, in Islam the early revival of the Greek heritage produced an intellectual renaissance that helped to define but did not radically transform the traditional order. Muslims continued to reject the belief in the self-sufficiency of the political community or in man as the measure of all things. An occasionalist, mystical and traditionalist intellectual orientation eventually prevailed in the Muslim world, providing a measure of stability but discouraging the sort of progress that was the child of the Age of Reason in the West. It is only in the latter part of the nineteenth century and in the twentieth century that the Muslim world, rudely awakened from its torpor by the impact of the modernized West, felt the pressing need for increased political integration and began groping for a more rationalist intellectual orientation. The Muslim world did not have time to evolve organically such instrumentalities of political integration as ideological parties and representative institutions. The attempt to transport political ideas and institutions ready-made from the West met with well-known difficulties that are still with us. Rapid political integration is a real challenge to man's ingenuity and ability to organize for common tasks, not only in the Muslim world but in all developing countries.

Appendices

A

Reception of Statutes of Government

The following examples illustrate the place that Māwardī's *Statutes of Government* (*al-Aḥkām al-sulṭanīyya*) occupied throughout Islamic history.

A book by the same name was written by Māwardī's younger contemporary, Abū Ya'lā ibn al-Farrā' (d. 1066), leader of the Ḥanbalites. This book is almost a word-for-word copy of Māwardī's and seems to have been prompted primarily by Māwardī's neglect of the Ḥanbalites in summarizing the various views of the juristic schools.

Under the Ayyūbids, 'Abd al-Raḥmān (d. 1193), in writing his book on politics for Saladin, reproduces the duties of the ruler from Māwardī without acknowledgement.[262]

The Mamlūk encyclopaedist Nuwayrī (d. 1332), in his *Nihāyat al-arab fī funūn al-adab*, depends very heavily on Māwardī's *Aḥkām* in discussing governnental offices that are required by the Law.

Ibn Jama'a (d. 1333) bases his *Taḥrīr al-aḥkām* to a large extent on Māwardī's book.

Ibn al-Ukhuwwa (d. 1329) begins his famous book on *ḥisba* with a copy of Māwardī's chapter on the subject.[263]

Ibn Khaldūn (d. 1406) states that he does not need to deal with the *shar'ī* statutes of government in detail because they have been fully set forth in works on this subject by eminent jurists such as Māwardī.[264]

The famous encyclopaedist, Qalqashandī, in urging the bureaucrats to know the requirements of the *sharī'a* in regard to various governmental offices, refers to Māwardī's book as containing the last word on the subject.[265]

The Ottoman Ṭāshköprüzāde (d. 1560), in discussing the administration of the army, states that there is nothing to add to Māwardī's coverage of this subject in his *Aḥkām*.[266]

In the age of imperialism, the Europeans, in their efforts to understand Islamic ideas on public law, translated Māwardī's *Aḥkām* into French and Dutch, and the part on judicial administration into English.[267]

Modern Muslim reformers often start with Māwardī without necessarily adhering specifically to his formulations. For example, Khayr al-Dīn al-Tūnisī (d. 1890) uses Māwardī's concept of delegation of authority as the basis for adopting representative institutions.[268]

The modernist Rashīd Riḍā, in discussing government in Islam, considers Māwardī's work the classical Muslim statement.[269]

Most modern works on Islamic political thought – those by Muslims are often programmatic – give Māwardī a prominent place.[270]

B
Biographical Note

Abū al-Ḥasan ʿAlī ibn Muḥammad ibn Ḥabīb al-Māwardī (AH 364–450/AD 975–1058) was born and grew up in Baṣra. The sources have little to offer about Māwardī's background, save that as a youth he was very friendly with Aḥmad ibn Abī al-Shawārib, a descendant of a famed family of jurists. Māwardī relates that their friendship was such that he regarded Ibn Abī al-Shawārib as a father and was regarded by him as a son. One can only speculate about the influence that this relationship might have had on Māwardī's future career at Baghdad,[271] for it is known that Ibn Abī al-Shawārib, six years after his appointment as judge of his native Baṣra, was summoned to Baghdad to fill the highest judicial office of chief judge (AH 405–17).[272]

After studying jurisprudence under Abū al-Qāsim al Ṣaymarī, an eminent Shāfiʿite jurist of Baṣra,[273] Māwardī was drawn to Baghdad, the seat of the caliphate and the greatest centre of Muslim learning. Although the date of his departure from Baṣra could not be determined exactly, it can be definitely placed before AH 398, for it is known that in Baghdad he studied under Abū Muḥammad ʿAbdullāh al-Bāfī (d. AH 398),[274] a learned jurist well versed in grammar and literature.

At Baghdad, Māwardī continued his juristic studies under the then most renowned Shāfiʿite jurist, Abū Ḥāmid al-Isfarāʾīnī (d. AH 406).[275] Needless to say, his traditional education included a thorough grounding in grammar, literature, Qur'an and Ḥadīth (traditions of the Prophet).

Māwardī held many judgeships in various parts of the Muslim lands,[276] and taught for a number of years in Baṣra and Baghdad.[277] Subkī mentions at least nine Shāfiʿites who studied either law or traditions under Māwardī.[278] An indication of Māwardī's eminent position in judicial circles of Baghdad can be found in the note that his son was the only *shāhid* (witness) whose testimony was received (AH 431) in Bayt al-Nawba. We are told that the chief judge, Ibn Mākūlā, followed this exceptional procedure out of respect for Māwardī.[279]

In addition to holding numerous judicial posts, Māwardī often served as emissary of the caliph to the various princes who were de facto rulers of the disintegrated Empire. Since this study is especially concerned with Māwardī's political thought, it is appropriate to summarize his political experiences and his relationship to both caliph and prince. The following chronological account of his political activities reveals Māwardī's devotion to the cause of the caliphate and his concern for effecting a modus vivendi between the various princes, on the one hand, and the princes and the caliph on the other. The previous sections have shown Māwardī's parallel efforts to salvage the position of the caliphate, symbol of the supremacy of the *sharīʿa* (Muslim Law), by reformulating the relationship between caliph and prince in the light of existing conditions.

Māwardī's active career spanned the caliphates of Qādir and Qā'im. The only mention of Māwardī's connection with the Caliph Qādir (d. AH 422) is a note by Yāqūt[280] that when the Caliph Qādir asked a leading jurist from each of the four schools of law to write a summary of jurisprudence, his choice fell on Māwardī to represent the Shāfiʿites. Māwardī thus wrote *al-Iqnāʿ*, for which the caliph had the highest praise.

In AH 422, the Caliph Qā'im, on succeeding his father, sent Māwardī to the Buwayhid prince, Abū Kālījār, to receive the oath of allegiance (*bayʿa*) and arrange for the *khuṭba* to the caliph.[281] The *khuṭba*, or recitation of the ruler's name in the Friday prayers, was the primary symbol of suzerainty. Māwardī's mission was successful. When asked by Abū Kālījār that the title 'The Great Sultan, Lord of the Nations' be conferred upon him, Māwardī managed to convince the Prince that such a title was befitting only to the caliph. On returning to Baghdad with magnificent gifts, Māwardī was given the task of reporting to Jalāl al-Dawla (the Buwayhid ruler of Baghdad, AH 416–34, who considered Abū Kālījār to be a serious threat).[282] Jalāl's fears were justified, for Abū Kālījār, in addition to holding Kirmān, Fāris and Khūzistān, had made definite headway in Iraq, where his name was recited in the *khuṭba* at both Baṣra and Kūfa.

Although a strong supporter of the caliph's cause, Māwardī also enjoyed the confidence of Jalāl al-Dawla. For example, we are told that in AH 427, when the army mutinied against Jalāl, seeking to expel him from Baghdad, Māwardī was among the three eminent jurists who were at Jalāl's residence, and whose advice as to the proper course of action was sought and heeded. The two other jurists were no less than Zaynabī, the *naqīb* (marshal) of the ʿAbbāsids, and Murtaḍā, the *naqīb* of the ʿAlids.[283]

In AH 428, Māwardī was one of the intermediaries who effected a conciliation between the two Buwayhid rulers, Jalāl al-Dawla and his nephew, Abū Kālījār.[284] The cause of the enmity between these two rulers, in addition to Abū Kālījār's infringement on Jalāl's territory in Iraq, was the existence among Jalāl's army in Baghdad of a strong faction who preferred the leadership of Abū Kālījār to the irresoluteness and incompetence of Jalāl.

In spite of his friendship with Jalāl al-Dawla, Māwardī, as illustrated by the following episode, was by no means subservient. Jalāl al-Dawla was granted by the caliph the additional title 'King of Kings'. When the preachers recited this title in the mosques on Friday, they were bombarded with bricks by the populace. This led the caliph to seek the legal opinions of some of the leading jurists. Māwardī held that such a title was befitting only to God and could not be applied to a worldly ruler. Apprehensive about his stand, which was different from the opinions of other jurists who were consulted, Māwardī ceased his daily visits to Jalāl al-Dawla. However, upon being summoned to the court by the Buwayhid prince, Māwardī discovered that his stand had won him greater esteem and was regarded by Jalāl as a sign of religious respect and impartiality.[285] It is interesting to note that, in the same year, Māwardī was given the honorific title 'Aqdā al-Qudāh', most eminent judge. The leading jurists of Baghdad, who had just sanctioned the title 'King of Kings', objected strongly to Māwardī's new honour, saying that no jurist ought to be given such a title. Their objection was not heeded and Māwardī held the title until his death.[286]

In AH 434, Māwardī was sent by the caliph to protest to Jalāl al-Dawla against the collection of *al-jawālī* (poll tax) that had gone customarily to the caliph. Jalāl admitted to Māwardī the necessity, in principle, of obedience to the caliph, but excused himself because of his bankruptcy and the incessant demands of the army. It was agreed that the caliph's agents would not be molested in collecting the *jawālī* the following year.[287]

Acting again as emissary for the caliph, Qā'im, Māwardī was sent (AH 435) to the Saljūqid Sulṭan Ṭughril who, in seizing the province of Rayy, had caused much destruction of life and property. Māwardī was to convey the caliph's disapproval of Ṭughril's behaviour and to exhort him to improve his treatment of the flock. He was also to bring about a concordat among Jalāl al-Dawla, Abū Kālījār and Ṭughril. Being the caliph's representative, Māwardī was received very cordially by Ṭughril.[288]

The main historical chronicles of this period make no reference to Māwardī's activity after AH 436. Māwardī died in AH 450 (AD 1058), three years after the Saljūqid Sulṭan, Ṭughril, entered Baghdad and put an end to the rule of the Buwayhid dynasty.

C

Listing of Works and Verification

No manuscripts are known to exist for the following three works of Māwardī:

1. *Amthāl al Qur'ān* (*Similes of the Qur'ān*)[289]
2. *al-Iqnāʿ* (*Convincement*). This is a summary of Shāfiʿite law written for the Caliph Qādir.[290]
3. *Kitāb fī al-naḥw* (*A Book on Grammar*). It is mentioned only by Yāqūt, who relates that he has seen this book.[291]

Furthermore, it is known that Māwardī wrote on the methodology of jurisprudence (*uṣūl al-fiqh*),[292] but no titles of such works of his could be traced. Nor could I find additional references to two books that Māwardī might have written, the one on the *sīra* (biography) and the other on the *khaṣā'is* (attributes) of the Prophet. We know of the former through a note in Māwardī's Aʿlām[293] where he expresses his intention of writing such a book; the only mention of the latter is in Sakhāwī's *Iʿlān*.[294]

For manuscripts and, in some cases, published editions of the following seven works (4–10), see Brockelmann's *Geschichte der Arabischen Litteratur*.[295]

4. *al-Nukat wa al-ʿuyūn fī tafsīr al-Qur'ān*[296] (*Exegesis of the Qur'ān: Major and Minor Themes*). Some authors have mistakenly listed *Tafsīr al-Qur'ān* and *al-Nukat wa al-ʿuyūn* as separate works.[297] A manuscript of the first volume of this exegesis of the Qur'ān was recently discovered in Yemen.[298]
5. *al-Hāwī fī furūʿ al-fiqh* (*A Comprehensive [Work] on Law*). In addition to the listings in *Geschichte der Arabischen Litteratur*, seven volumes of this work, formerly in the Landberg Collection, are now at Yale University.[299] *Al-Kāfī fi sharḥ mukhtaṣar al-Muzanī* (*Competent Commentary on Muzani's Compendium*), which is mentioned only by Subkī,[300] is no other than *al-Ḥāwi*, as Māwardī himself clearly indicates.[301]
6. *Aʿlām al nubuwwa* (*Signs of Prophethood*). This book is also known as *Dalā'il al nubuwwa*[302] (*Proofs of Prophethood*).
7. *al-Amthāl wa al ḥikam* (*Proverbs and Wise Sayings*). This is listed as such only by Ibn al-Jawzī.[303]
8. *al-Aḥkām al sulṭāniyya* (*Ordinances of Government*).
9. *Adab al-dunyā wa al-dīn* (*Proper Conduct Befitting this World and Religion*).

10. *Tashīl al-naẓar wa taʿjīl al-ẓafar** (*Facilitating Administration and Hastening Success*). Yāqūt substitutes *naṣr* (victory) for *naẓar*.[304] I think that *naẓar* is more appropriate since it rhymes with *ẓafar*.

My research supplements the *Geschichte der Arabischen Litteratur* in regard to the following four listings.

The Istanbul manuscript, *Adab al-qāḍī*† (*Rules and Morals Relating to the Office of Judge*), listed in *Geschichte der Arabischen Litteratur* as a separate book, was found to be a part of Māwardī's *al-Ḥāwī*.

The manuscripts on *ḥisba* (supervision of markets and morals) are not Māwardī's. The Jerusalem[305] and the Istanbul[306] manuscripts are copies of the same work and, on comparison, were found to be identical with Ibn al-Ukhuwwa's book[307] on the same subject.[308] Clearly, parts of these manuscripts were written much later than Māwardī's time. The first theoretical part of the book is a word-for-word copy of Māwardī's chapter on *ḥisba* in *al-Aḥkām*, hence the mistaken attribution of the whole manuscript to Māwardī. The practical part is an appropriation of Shayzarī's book on *ḥisba*[309] supplemented by thirty additional chapters. It is clear, then, why the Arabic sources do not attribute a separate work on *ḥisba* to Māwardī.

The rest of this section will be devoted to supporting the following hypotheses. The work listed in *Geschichte der Arabischen Litteratur* as *Qawānīn al-wizāra wa siyāsat al-mulk* is:

11. *Qawānīn al wizāra* (*Rules of the Wazīrate*), to be discussed below. Māwardī did not write a book entitled *Naṣīḥat al-mulūk* (*Advice to Kings*). The Paris manuscript[310] listed as *Naṣīḥat al-mulūk* is Māwardī's but bears an incorrect title. Its correct title should be:
12. *Siyāsat al-mulk*‡ (*'Political' Administration*).

* *Tashīl al-naẓar* is considered the most important book by Māwardī concerning the theory of the state, while his *al-Aḥkām al-sulṭāniyya* is considered as a summary of his concepts of the Islamic State and its institutions. An edition of *Tashīl al-naẓar*, critically edited by Muhammad Jassem al-Hadithi, was published in Baghdad, while another, critically edited by Ridwan al-Sayyed, was published in 1987 in Beirut.

† Muhyi Hilal al-Sarhan published *Adab al-qāḍī*, extracted from his *al-Ḥāwī*, in Baghdad in four volumes. In 1993, *al-Ḥāwī* as a whole was published by Dar al-Kutub al-Ilmiyya, Beirut.

‡ *Naṣīḥat al-mulūk*, which the author calls *Siyāsat al-mulk*, was published three times, critically edited by Muhammad Jassem al-Hadithi, Khidr Muhammad Khidr and Fu'ād Abd al-Munʿim Ahmad respectively. There is one main difficulty in the book, which Fu'ād Abd al-Munʿim was aware of. He noticed that the juridical perceptions that

All references to Māwardī's *Naṣīḥat al-mulūk* are based, directly or indirectly, on the Paris manuscript. This is the case even with the puzzling note occurring in Ḥājjī Khalīfa's *Kashf* (Turkish edition only). Appearing under the entry 'Naṣīḥat al-mulūk' is the distorted insert 'wa lil-Māwardī fī mu'īd al-ni'am' (and [a book by this title is] by al-Māwardī in *Mu'īd al ni'am*). Thorough examination of *Mu'id al-ni'am*[311] revealed no mention of *Naṣīḥat al-mulūk*. The source of this insert was finally traced to the catalogue of the Arabic books at the Bibliothèque Nationale where *Naṣīḥat al-mulūk* is sub-listed under the same number as two other works, one of which is *Mu'īd al-ni'am*.

The Paris manuscript is dated AH 1007 (AD 1598), five centuries after Māwardī's time; and the author and title page, as well as the biographical note on Māwardī at the end of the manuscript, are written in a later hand than the body of the manuscript. These facts, coupled with the absence of any reference, other than the Paris manuscript, to a work by Māwardī entitled *Naṣīḥat al-mulūk*, call for a verification of Māwardī's authorship .

First, we know that Māwardī did concern himself with problems of government and administration. These he treated in a number of works, for example his 'mirror for princes', *Tashīl al-naẓar wa ta'jīl al-ẓafar*.

Stylistically, this manuscript bears strong resemblance to other works by Māwardī, and its content parallels Māwardī's views as expressed elsewhere. The authors mentioned in the *Naṣīḥa* work are primarily those referred to elsewhere by Māwardī, and roughly forty lines of the poetry quoted in *Naṣīḥa* appear in Māwardī's other books. Even the Mu'tazilite leanings of the author[312] can be viewed as supporting evidence, for Māwardī often evinced such tendencies.[313]

Furthermore, an examination of the *Naṣīḥa* manuscript indicates that the date of its composition is about Māwardī's time. Of the large number of quotations in this manuscript, the latest that I could trace is

---

appear incidentally in the text tend to be Hanafite, while Māwardī was Shafiite, as is clear in *al-Ḥāwī*, *al-Iqnaa'* and *al-Aḥkām al-sulṭāniyya*. But the political views that appear in the book, the proverbs and poems and the stylistic features are similar to what we know of Māwardī in *Tashīl al-naẓar* and *Qawānīn al-wizāra*, yet the analysis here is easier than that in the other books. Likewise, the form of advice which intervenes in many stories is the rule. As for the title, and whether the correct one is *Siyāsat al-mulk* or *Naṣīḥat al-mulūk*, it seems that the copyist did not know the title of the manuscript and so gave it the title *Naṣīḥat al-mulūk* depending on his reading of it, and noticing that it belongs to the kind of literature known as 'Mirrors of Princes'. But the author's assertion that the title of the book should be *Siyāsat al-mulk* remains in question.

a stanza of poetry[314] attributed by Tha'ālibī[315] to Ibn Khālawayh (d. 370/980).[316] Giving examples of good rulers in another place in the manuscript, the author states: 'and thus were the Sāmānid kings'.[317] This may be taken as an indication that the time of writing was after the fall of the Sāmānids, AD 999.

Finally, a very significant reference occurs in Māwardī's *Adab al-dunyā wa al-dīn*. In discussing the various kinds of human occupations, he lists as a separate group those occupations which involve activities based on 'sound opinions, such as government (*siyāsa*) of people and administration (*tadbīr*) of the realm'. He omits any discussion of this type of occupation on the grounds that he had 'devoted a separate book to the subject of *siyāsa*'.[318] This quotation could have referred to *Tashīl* had it not been for the fact that the statement in *Adab al-dunyā wa al-dīn* antedates *Tashīl* by many years.[319] The preceding description of a book treating *siyāsa* and *tadbīr* well fits the contents of the *Naṣīḥa* manuscript, where the words *siyāsa* or *tadbīr* occur specifically in the titles of five of the ten chapters.

The above considerations point to Māwardī's authorship of the Paris manuscript described as *Naṣīḥat al-mulūk*. Māwardī's work on the *wizāra* is a fifty-seven-page booklet that discusses the rights and duties of the *wazīr*, distinguishing between the *wizāra*s of *tafwīḍ* (unlimited delegation of authority) and *tanfīdh* (limited execution). The shorter title, *Qawānīn al-wizāra*, seems far more appropriate for the limited scope of this work. Indeed, many authors[320] list *Qawānīn al-wizāra* as a title of one of Māwardī's books without any mention of 'Siyāsat al-mulk', and Ḥājjī Khalīfa[321] and others after him[322] specifically list *Siyāsat al-mulk* as a separate work.

Even the Cairo publisher gives Māwardī's work the descriptive title *Adab al wazīr*, and merely claims that it is known as *Qawānīn al-wizāra wa siyāsat al-mulk*. Furthermore, the catalogues of three of the four libraries where manuscripts of this work of Māwardī on the wazīrate are known to exist do not include 'Siyāsat al-mulk' in the title; the fourth manuscript (formerly in the possession of Landberg, and now at Yale University) was copied as late as AH 1289 (AD 1872), and the addition of 'Siyāsat al-mulk' to the title could be the work of the copyist.

Why should 'Siyāsat al-mulk' occur in the title of the Yale manuscript and the subtitle of the Cairo published work? Ibn Khallikān[323] and some later authors,[324] in enumerating Māwardī's works, place 'Siyāsat al-mulk' after 'Qawānīn al-Wizāra'. The absence of punctuation marks in the Arabic manuscripts and the repetition of the conjunction 'and' make it unclear whether the above titles refer to one or two books. This, I feel, is the source of the confusion.

The preceding discussion supports two points: that Māwardī is the author of the Paris manuscript described as 'Naṣīḥat al mulūk', and that he had written a book entitled *Siyāsat al-mulk*. It remains to show that the Paris manuscript is, in fact, Māwardī's *Siyāsat al-mulk*.

First, the title *Siyāsat al-mulk* describes very well the content of the Paris manuscript. Second, the published Arabic sources list under the title *Naṣīḥat al-mulūk* no work other than Ghazzāli's.[325] One might well ask how then the title *Naṣīḥat al-mulūk* was given to this manuscript of Māwardī. The title of the book is not specifically mentioned in the text. As stated previously, the title page of the *Naṣīḥa* is clearly written later than the actual text. I believe that the recorded title, *Naṣīḥat al-mulūk*, is based on the following sentence at the end of the text: 'tamma kitāb naṣīḥat al-mulūk' ('here ends the book of *Advice to Kings*'). This sentence appears to be an addition of the original copyist, who extrapolated from the stated purpose of the author. For, at the outset, the author notes that he has written this 'naṣīḥatan lil-mulūk'[326] (in order to advise kings).

The above considerations, while inconclusive when taken separately, collectively justify my conclusions which in turn offer an explanation of the known data.

Notes

1. For a discussion of the relation of reason to revelation in Christendom, see Etienne Gilson, *Reason and Revelation in the Middle Ages*. (Footnotes are given in abbreviated form. For detailed information, consult Bibliography.)
2. It is significant that the tenth-century Muslim philosopher Fārābī, in classifying the sciences (*Iḥsā' al-ʿulūm*, p. 102), lumps theology and jurisprudence together with politics in the Greek sense.
3. For example, Ṭāshöprüzāde in discussing books on prophecy states that no work is better or more beneficial than Māwardī's *Proofs of Prophecy* (*Miftāḥ al-saʿāda*, I, 263).
4. See Appendix A.
5. For a general discussion, see A. J. Arberry, *Revelation and Reason in Islam*.
6. Baghdādī, *Uṣūl al-dīn*, pp. 6–7; Abū Yaʿlā ibn al-Farrā', *al-Muʿtamad fī uṣūl al-dīn*, fol. 1b.
7. Baghdādī, op. cit., pp. 11–12; Abū Yaʿlā, op. cit., fol. 1b; Māwardī, *Aʿlam*, p. 14.
8. Ibn al-Muqaffaʿ, *al-Adab al-ṣaghīr*, pp. 29–30. [Most scholars now suggest that *al-Adab al-ṣaghīr* by Ibn al-Muqaffaʿ is not a separate book, but is rather a selection from his works gathered on a common basis.]
9. Ibid., p. 30.
10. Ibid., p. 32.
11. Most of the Falāsifa would agree with Ibn Rushd's position expressed in *Faṣl al-maqāl*, pp. 14–15.
12. See, for example, Fārābī's patronizing statement in *al-Jamʿ bayn ra'y al-ḥakīmayn*, p. 104.
13. Kindī, 'Fī al-falsafa al-'ūlā', *Rasā'il*, p. 97.
14. Ibid., pp. 103–4.
15. E.g., Fārābī, *Fuṣūl al-madanī*, p. 136; Ibn Sīnā, 'Fī aqsam al-ʿulūm al-'aqliyya', in *Tisʿ rasā'il*, p. 115.
16. Ghazzālī, *Faḍā'iḥ al-Bāṭiniyya*, pp. 3, 9.
17. *Rasā'il*.
18. Tawḥīdī, *Imtāʿ*, II, 18.
19. Ibid., II, 6–7.
20. Ibid., III, 187.
21. Although he eventually supported the Traditionalists against the Muʿtazila, the Caliph Qādir had earlier in his reign supported handsomely the Muʿtazilite ʿAlī ibn Saʿīd al-Iṣṭakhrī for his polemical work against extreme Shīʿīs (Ibn al-Jawzī, *Muntaẓam*, VII, 268).
22. The Ashʿarites did not always agree with their eponym.
23. E.g., Ibn Baṭṭa al-ʿUkbarī, *al-Ibāna*.
24. *Al-Muʿtamad fī usūl al-dīn*.
25. G. Makdisi, 'Ashʿarī and the Ashʿarites in Islamic Religious History', *Studia Islamica*, XVII (1962), pp. 37–80; XVIII (1963), pp. 19–40.
26. This is the essence of Qushayrī's *Risāla*. Just as Ghazzālī did not

want the *sharī'a* to disregard Ṣūfism, Qushayrī did not want Ṣūfism to disregard the *sharī'a*.

27. Māwardī, *A'lām*, pp. 3–6.
28. In spite of their formally rationalist structure, Māwardī's epistemological views are not very different from those of the Ash'arites. See, for example, the works of his two older Ash'arite contemporaries, Bāqillani (*Tamhīd*, pp. 7–13) and Baghdādī (*Uṣūl al-dīn*, pp. 11–15).
29. Māwardī, *A'lām*, pp. 6–10.
30. For other proofs, see A. J. Wensinck, 'Les Preuves de l'existence de Dieu dans la théologie musulmane, *'Koninklijke Akademie van Wetenschappen*, Vol. 81, Ser. A., No. 2. See also the proof by Bāqillānī in *Tamhīd*, pp. 44–500. Compare Māwardī's proof with the following argument of Ibn al-Muqaffa' – middle of the eighth century: the consensus of both learned and ignorant is that God does exist. Those who still have doubts would have to grant that they were created in time and that they did not create themselves; therefore, they would have to admit the existence of a Creator. Furthermore, let them consider the mustard seed, they will realize that 'it has in charge of it One who causes it to sprout and grow, assigns it its nourishment from earth and water, and sets the time for its germination and death' (*al-Adab al-Ṣaghir*, p. 32).
31. Ṭāshköprüzāde, *Miftaḥ al-sa'āda*, I, 263.
32. Māwardī, *A'lām*, pp. 35–8.
33. Ibid., pp. 13–26.
34. This is the Ash'arite position.
35. This is the Mu'tazilite position.
36. This differs from the Judeo-Christian Biblical tradition.
37. Māwardī, *A'lām*, p. 36.
38. Māwardī, *Adab al-dunyā*, pp. 3, 29; Māwardī, *A'lām*, pp. 13, 14.
39. Māwardī, *A'lām*, p. 16.
40. Ibid., p. 14.
41. Māwardī, *Adab*, p. 29.
42. Ibid. A similar view is expressed in Māwardī, *A'lām*, p. 11.
43. Māwardī, *A'lām*, p. 15.
44. Ibid., p. 16.
45. Māwardī, *Tashīl*, fol. 30b. Māwardī expresses similar views elsewhere: *Adab*, pp. 29, 120; *A'lām*, pp. 11, 13, 16.
46. Māwardī, *Adab*, p. 38.
47. Māwardī, *A'lām*, pp. 11, 13, 16.
48. Ibid., p. 16.
49. Māwardī, *Tashīl*, fol. 30b.
50. Māwardī, *Adab*, p. 120.
51. E.g., Yāqūt reports that Māwardī was considered a Mu'tazilite in *uṣūl*, but adds that he is in no position to confirm or deny the allegation (Yāqūt, *Irshād*, V, 407); Subkī quotes Ibn Ṣalāḥ, who accused Māwardī of being a veiled Mu'tazilite, without attempting to exonerate Māwardī from such a charge (Subkī, *Ṭabaqāt*, III, 303). Rescher, in his introduction to the German translation of *Adab al-dunyā wa al-dīn*, claims that Māwardī was a Mu'tazilite.
52. H. A. R. Gibb implies that Māwardī was an Ash'arite ('Some Considerations on the Sunni Theory of the Caliphate', *Studies on the Civilization of Islam*, p. 142).

53. Had Māwardī professed Mu'tazilism, he could not have held a judicial post in Baghdad. See Ibn al-Jawzī, *Muntaẓam*, VIII, 25, where in AH 417 Ṣaymarī had to disclaim Mu'tazilism before he could be accepted as official witness by the Chief Judge.
54. Neither Ibn 'Asākir (*Tabyīn*, p. 447) nor Subkī (Ṭabaqāt, II, 254–8) counts Māwardī among the followers of Ash'arī. Similarly, Ibn al-Murtaḍā, in the section of *al-Munya wa al-amal* that lists the Mu'tazilites, does not mention Māwardī.
55. When he was warned by a Traditionalist against innovating, Māwardī replied that he was a *mujtahid* and not a *muqallid* (Yāqūt, *Irshād*, V, 407).
56. See quote from Ibn Ṣalāh in Subkī's *Ṭabaqāt*, III, 303.
57. Māwardī, *A'lām*, pp. 11–13; Māwardī, *Adab*, p. 79.
58. Ash'arī, *Ibāna*, p. 59.
59. For an Ash'arite view, see Baghdādī, *Uṣūl*, p. 149; Baqillānī, *Tamhīd*, p. 97.
60. This is the commonly used name for extreme Shī'īs.
61. E.g., holders of rival theological views often belonged to the same school of law.
62. For example, after the thirteenth-century Suhrāwardī, Ibn al-'Arabī and Mullā Ṣadrā were far more popular than Kindī, Fārābī or Ibn Sīnā.
63. The name Murji'a is usually given to those who, unlike the Khārijites, refuse to consider a sinner an unbeliever but give him hope by postponing (*irjā'*) judgment until the Last Judgment.
64. Ibn al-Muqaffa', *al-Adab al-kabīr*, p. 75.
65. Ibn al-Muqaffa', *Risālat al-ṣaḥāba*, p. 157.
66. Ibn al-Muqaffa', *al-Adab al-kabīr*, p. 75.
67. H. A. R. Gibb, 'An Interpretation of Islamic History', *Studies on the Civilization of Islam*, p. 12.
68. Abū Yūsuf, *Kitāb al-Kharāj*, p. 4.
69. Ibn Ziyān, *Wāsitat al-sulūk fī siyāsat al-mulūk*, pp. 119–20.
70. Ibn Qutayba, *Ta'wīl mukhtalif al-ḥadīth*, p. 4.
71. I am convinced that Ibn Abī al-Rabī''s *Suluk al-mālik fī tadbīr al-mamālik* was written around 840 and not in the thirteenth century as Zaydān, Goldziher, Brockelman, Ritter, Plessner and Dunlop allege. I hope to spell out the reasons for my conclusion on a more appropriate occasion. [Yet recent research proves that the book was a late work. Ibn Abī al-Rabi' copied two chapters from *Tashīl al-naẓar wa ta'jīl al-ẓafar* by Māwardī (AH 450/AD 1058).]
72. Ibn Abī al-Rabī', *Sulūk* p. 8.
73. Tawhīdī, *Imtā'*, II, 116–17.
74. Bīrunī, *Āthār*, p. 132.
75. Tawḥīdī, *Imtā'*, II, 33.
76. Ikhwān, *Rasā'il*, IV, 32
77. E.g., ibid., I, 132.
78. Ibid., IV, 225, 242.
79. Yāqūt, *Irshād*, V, 407.
80. Māwardī, *Aḥkām*, pp. 431–2.
81. The work bearing the same title, by the leader of the Ḥanbalites, Māwardī's younger contemporary Abū Ya'lā ibn al-Farrā', is principally a reproduction of Māwardī's book with the addition of

Ḥanbalite references. Māwardī's neglect of the Ḥanbalites in his survey of the opinions of the various legal schools is probably due to his aversion to Ḥanbalite fundamentalism.

82. Since the relation of *sharī'a* to government was an overriding concern of Māwardī in his various writings, the following discussion will be based on all of Māwardī's extant books and manuscripts.
83. Māwardī, *Adab*, pp. 117–18.
84. Ibid., p. 116.
85. Ibid., p. 121.
86. Ibid., p. 120.
87. Ibid., p. 121.
88. Māwardī, *Tashīl*, fol. 30b.
89. Māwardī, *Adab*, p. 122.
90. Ibid., pp. 121–2.
91. Ibid., p. 122.
92. Ibid.
93. The choice of the term 'imāma' rather than *khilāfa* is characteristic of most writings on this subject and stems primarily from the fact that Sunnīs were usually writing in response to the polemics of the Shī'īs, who employed the term 'imām' rather than *khalīfa* in referring to their supreme religious and political leader.
94. For a serious analysis, see Professor Gibb's article 'Al-Māwardī's Theory of the Caliphate', in his *Studies on the Civilization of Islam*, pp. 151–65.
95. Many writers, in order to reinforce the caliph's declining authority, emphasized the importance of obedience and the serious consequences of disobedience by designating the caliph vicegerent of God. Māwardī rejected this designation because it implied too great a power for the ruler. When in another context (*Siyāsa*, fol. 8b) he encounters the current saying that 'the caliph is the shadow of God on earth', Māwardī explains it in such a way as to underline not the caliph's power but his responsibility to imitate God's justice. [The author refers here and many times afterwards to *Naṣīḥat al-mulūk*, related to Māwardī, and calls it *Siyāsat al-mulk*. Fu'ād 'Abd al-Mun'im Ahmad, who published the book in 1987, noted that most of the jurisprudential ideas which appear in the book have an inclination to the Hanafi faith, while Māwardī was Shafiite, as is well known. As for the political ideas, they are similar to those which appear in Māwardī's other books, *Tashīl al-naẓar* and *Qawānīn al-wizāra* in particular.
96. Versus Khārijites.
97. The consensus of the community (i.e. the men of religion) is what makes the setting-up of an imām a religious obligation. Contrary to E. I. J. Rosenthal (*Political Thought in Medieval Islam*, p. 28) the consensus of the community is not required to make the contract of the imāma binding.
98. In *Aḥkām*, pp. 3, 4, and *Adab*, p. 122, Māwardī merely lists the two positions – the one holding the imāma obligatory by reason, the other by revelation – without taking sides.
99. For Māwardī's position, that the spheres of reason and revelation are not mutually exclusive but are overlapping, see Part One (Reason and Revelation) above.

100. Professor Gibb is thus wrong in attributing to Māwardī the position that 'the imāma is obligatory by revelation, not by reason' (*Studies on the Civilization of Islam*, p. 155). E. I. J. Rosenthal (*Political Thought in Medieval Islam*, p. 28) makes the same mistake. Those who held that the imāma was obligatory by revelation only were the Ash'arites (Baghdādī, *Uṣūl*, p. 272) and the Traditionalists, who held that reason does not lead to knowledge of legal requirements (Ibn al-Farrā', *Aḥkām*, p. 4).
101. Māwardī, *Aḥkām*, pp. 9, 11.
102. Ibn al-Farrā' quotes hadīths, ascribed to Aḥmad ibn Ḥanbal, that dispense with the requirements of probity and learning (*Aḥkām*, p. 4).
103. That such designation needs further ratification (the opinion of some *'ulamā'* of Baṣra) is summarily dismissed. Rosenthal's statement that 'it is unanimously held that the office-holder possesses authority only if he is confirmed in office by the *ijmā'* of the community' (*Political Thought*, p. 37) is misleading. Rosenthal is also incorrect in claiming (ibid., p. 30) that Māwardī ignored Umayyid and 'Abbāsid practice. While he insists that the office of caliph, even though limited to the tribe of Quraysh, must not be automatically passed on from father to son, Māwardī does allow the caliph to designate a qualified successor. As for the historical practice of designating one's own son as heir apparent, Māwardī finds himself unable either to sanction the practice (Ibn al-Farrā' does, *Aḥkām*, p. 9), for it smacks of thinly-veiled inheritance, or to reject it outright, because that would be to play into the hands of the Shī'īs, who attacked the political constitution of the Muslim community.
104. Ibn al-Farrā', unlike Māwardī, does not attempt to rationalize the historical process. On the one hand he insists that the contract of the imāma, to be valid, must be concluded by all those who loosen and bind, and on the other hand, he accepts frankly the imāma of whoever wins by force if he is consequently given the allegiance (*bay'a*) of the community (*Mu'tamad*, fol. 95a). By *bay'a*, Ibn al-Farrā' seems to mean the tacit consent rather than the positive pledge of the community. Similarly, election by all those who loosen and bind is used as a negative principle to invalidate the contract by one or a few electors – Ash'arite and Mu'tazilite positions respectively.
105. See previous note.
106. The word *adab* has various usages; it may be translated as 'proper conduct'. *Adab* works addressed to the rulers can be translated as 'mirrors for princes'.
107. Pseudo-Jāḥiẓ, *al-Tāj*, p. 66.
108. Māwardī, *Tashīl*, fol. 1b.
109. Ibid.
110. Abū Ḥanīfa holds that what an apostate had earned while a Muslim may be inherited; and Abū Yūsuf, that all his wealth may be inherited (Māwardī, *Aḥkām*, p. 91).
111. *Ḥudūd* are severe legal penalties, such as stoning or cutting-off of the hand, that are prescribed for specific criminal offences.
112. Māwardī, *Aḥkām*, pp. 96–7. This is somewhat different from

Māwardī's position expressed in *Ḥāwī* (XVII, fol. 259a), where fighting is considered permissible to ensure the unity of the community.

113. Māwardī, *Aḥkām*, p. 10.
114. Ibid., p. 97.
115. The Dhimmīs are the inhabitants of the conquered territories who, because they were the possessors of previous revelations, were permitted to practise their religion and to run their local communities, but were subject to certain obligations such as the payment of a poll tax.
116. H. F. Amedroz has written articles on Māwardī's discussion of the offices of *qāḍī*, *maẓālim* and *ḥisba* that were useful in translation (*Journal of the Royal Asiatic Society*, 1910, pp. 761–96; 1911, pp. 635–74; 1916, pp. 77–101, 287, 314).
117. A slave cannot hold a delegated office, but he may give fatwas (legal opinions).
118. Abū Ḥanīfa allows women to adjudicate in limited matters; Ṭabarī puts women on a footing of equality with men (Māwardī, *Aḥkām*, p. 107).
119. Māwardī goes as far as asserting that the customary appointment of non-Muslims as judges over their coreligionists (sanctioned by Abū Ḥanīfa) is strictly an executive rather than judicial appointment. A non-Muslim may reject such jurisdiction, in which case he falls under the jurisdiction of the Muslim judge (Māwardī, *Aḥkām*, pp. 108–9).
120. Inborn reason, adequate for legal responsibility, is not enough.
121. Probity is required in holders of all delegated offices.
122. Abū Hanīfa is less strict in this regard (ibid., p. 110).
123. The appointment to judicial office of one who does not accept traditions related by individual reporters is not permissible, for his stand constitutes a rejection of a fundamental principle that has been agreed upon by the companions of the Prophet, and that is the basis of most ordinances of the Law.
124. It seems that Māwardī, like some Shāfi'ites, would allow the appoitment of Ẓahirites to judicial office, for even though they deny the value of analogy (*qiyās*) in theory, they do use individual interpretation in practice.
125. E.g., governor, military commander or head of police.
126. 'This, though we detest it, is admissible' (Māwardī, *Aḥkam*, p. 377).
127. In fact Māwardī makes one exception, and gives the police the right to imprison for life a criminal who is not restrained by the legal penalties and persists in his criminal acts.
128. I.e., *al-Aḥkām al-sulṭāniyya*.
129. A *wazīr tanfīdh* may be neither free nor Muslim (certain traditions ascribed to Ibn Ḥanbal would exclude *dhimmīs*) and need not have knowledge of the Law or financial and military affairs. A generation later, Juwaynī is extremely critical of Māwardī for allowing a *dhimmī* to hold this office (*Ghiyāth al-umam*, fol. 18a).
130. Māwardī, *Qawānīn*, p. 43. [Ridwan al-Sayyed critically edited *Qawānīn al-wizāra wa siyāsat al-mulk*, referring to new manuscripts. It was published twice, in 1979 and 1993.]
131. Māwardī, *Aḥkām*, p. 31 (my italics).

132. The expanded duties would include religious, legal and financial administration.
133. Ibid., p. 56.
134. Following Professor Gibb ('Some Considerations on the Sunni Theory of the Caliphate', first published in 1938 and republished in *Studies on the Civilization of Islam*), these positions are usually illustrated by Ibn Jamā'a (d. 1333) and Ghazzālī (d. 1111) respectively. It seems to me that Professor Gibb is forcing a pattern when he sees a continuous trend of increasing concessions to power culminating in Ibn Jamā'a's position. The crucial importance of power (*shawka*) in the appointment and deposition of caliphs was clearly perceived by Ghazzālī's teacher, Juwaynī (*Ghiyāth al-umum*, fol. 35a). A generation before Juwaynī, Ibn al-Farrā' had already accepted the imāma of whoever holds power and has the acquiescence of the community (*Mu'tamad*, fol. 95a). Even two centuries befor Juwaynī, Aḥmad ibn Ḥanbal had conceded that the caliphate belonged to whoever won the struggle for power.
135. E.g., Ghazzālī, Ibn Taymiyya, Taftāzānī.
136. 'Constitutional Organization', *Law in the Middle East*, p. 23.
137. 'Taḥrīr al-aḥkām', *Islamica*, VI, 361–2.
138. This contradicts A. K. S. Lambton's conclusion ('Justice in the Medieval Persian Theory of Kingship', *Studia Islamica*, XVII [1962], pp. 91–119) that the criterion of justice is peculiar to 'medieval' as contrasted with 'classical' Islamic political thought.
139. 'Āmirī, *al-Sa'āda wa al-is'ād*, p. 223.
140. See, for example, Miskawayh, *Risāla fī māhiyyat al-'adl*, p. 19, and Ibn Khaldun, *Muqaddima*, II, 516–17.
141. Māwardī, *Adab*, pp. 210, 212.
142. Ibid., p. 192.
143. Ibid., p. 129.
144. E.g., the twelfth-century writer 'Abd al-Raḥmān al-Shayzarī. See his *al-Manhaj al-maslūk*, pp. 222–3.
145. Ṭurṭūshī (d. 1226 or 1231) makes the distinction between divine justice which is expressed in the Muslim revelation and conventional justice which is not limited to any religious community (*Sirāj al-mulūk*, pp. 96–9). When the word ''adl' is used in Muslim political writings, it almost always refers to what Ṭurṭūshī calls conventional justice.
146. Thus, while to Augustine a non-Christian polity cannot be called just, to Muslims a non-Muslim polity can enjoy conventional justice and, before the coming of Islam, a measure of divine justice if such polity possessed a revealed message. However, after the coming of Islam, the most perfect manifestation of divine justice is to be found only in a Muslim polity.
147. Māwardī, *Siyāsat al-mulk*, fol. 16a.
148. Māwardī, *Qawānīn al-wizāra*, p. 12.
149. Māwardī would agree to Ibn Khaldūn's addition (*Muqaddima*, II, 683–5) of fair prices and opposition to monopolies.
150. Māwardī, *Aḥkām*, pp. 136–8.
151. Māwardī, *Qawānīn al-wizāra*, p. 12.
152. This was especially the case in the area of politics. For example, the fourteenth-century sultan, Ibn Ziyān (d. 1352), in advising his son

on the requirements for successful rule, distinguished two criteria: custom and religious Law. Perfect justice is in observing both criteria, tyranny in their disregard. The ruler's neglect of custom would lead to ruin, but his observance of custom, even given partial disregard of the religious requirement, would ensure his rule. Ibn Ziyān points out that the latter practice is that of many a king of his time, and calls it intermediary justice.

153. See pp. 23–5 above.
154. Jāḥiz, *'Uthmāniyya*, pp. 251–2.
155. 'Abd al-Raḥmān Badawī (ed.), ''Ahd al-malik ilā ibnih', *al-Usūl al-yūnāniyya lil-naẓarāt al-siyāsiyya fī al-islām*, p. 22. Badawī attributes the work to Aḥmad ibn Yūsuf ibn Ibrāhīm (d. ca. 942).
156. Ibid.
157. Ṭurṭūshī, *Sirāj al-mulūk*, p. 3.
158. The reference is to the Sassanids.
159. Ṭurṭūshī, *Sirāj*, pp. 96, 97. The Arabic term for divine justice is *''adl ilāhī'*. Ṭurṭūshī uses this interchangably with *''adl nabawī'* (prophetic justice).
160. Ibid., pp. 4, 96–100.
161. Ibid., pp. 96–9. Ṭurṭūshī does not specifically use the term 'conventional justice', but writes that justice is divided into two parts: the first is divine or prophetic justice, the second is equivalent to conventional government (*siyāsa iṣṭilāḥiyya*). The variant *'siyāsa iṣlāḥiyya'* (good government) also occurs in the edited text.
162. See, for example: ibid., p. 96; Ibn 'abd Rabbih, *al-'Iqd al-farīd*, I, 39; Yaḥyā ibn al-Biṭrīq, 'al-Siyāsa fī tadbīr al-ri'āsa', in Badawī (ed.), *al-Uṣūl al-yūnāniyya*, I, 126.
163. Ghazzālī, *Naṣīhat al-mulūk*, p. 40.
164. Māwardī, *Siyāsat al-mulk*, fol. 97.
165. Ibid., fol. 16a.
166. E.g., Pseudo Jāḥiẓ (ninth century), *al-Tāj*, pp. 67–8; al-Ḥasan ibn 'Abd Allāh al-'Abbāsī (fourteenth century), *Āthār al-uwal fī tartīb al-duwal*, p. 41.
167. F. Rosenthal, 'State and Religion according to Abū al-Ḥasan al-'Āmirī', *Islamic Quarterly*, III (1956), p. 52.
168. This is what Walter Ullmann calls the descending conception (W. Ullmann, *Principles of Government and Politics in the Middle Ages*, p. 20.
169. For an illustration of this view, see the statement by the famous fifteenth-century encyclopaedist, Ibshīhī, in his *al-Mustaṭraf fī kull fann mustaẓraf*, I, 144.
170. Māwardī, *Qawānīn*, p. 48; Māwardī, *Siyāsa*, fol. 56b.
171. Māwardī, *Tashīl*, fol. 43a. Such appointments were not uncommon in Māwardī's time. See, e.g., Ibn al-Jawzī, *Muntaẓam*, VIII, 54.
172. Māwardī, *Aḥkām*, p. 138.
173. Māwardī, *Siyāsa*, fol. 56b.
174. Māwardī, *Aḥkām*, p. 138.
175. Māwardī, *Tashīl*, fol. 54b.
176. Māwardī, *Qawānīn*, p. 37.
177. Māwardī, *Aḥkām*, p. 136.
178. Ibid., pp. 135–8.
179. The most extreme demand for submission was made by the

Fāṭimid ideologue, al-Qāḍī al-Nuʿmān (d. 974), who required voluntary submission to the imām in deed, word and intention even if such submission should involve destruction of the believer's property or life (*Kitāb al-himma fī ādāb atbāʿ al-aʾimma*, pp. 38–9, 74.

180. The advocacy of the principle of tyrannicide occurs in Ibn Sīnā's *Ilāhiyyāt*, p. 452: 'The lawgiver ought to decree in his law that it is the duty of all the citizens to fight and slay whoever rebels and claims the caliphate by virtue of force or wealth; he should declare lawful the blood of anyone who, although able, does not fulfil this duty ...; and he must stipulate that next to belief in the Prophet nothing would bring man closer to God than tyrannicide'.
181. These three recur constantly in all classifications of Muslim sects (e.g. those by Ibn Qutayba, pseudo-Nawbakhtī, Ashʿarī, Khwārizmī, Ibn al-Nadīm, Muqaddasī, Baghdādī, Ibn Ḥazm and Shahrastānī). It is from among the various other sects that the 'ahl al-Sunna' eventually emerge and prevail.
182. This schematic presentation is based largely on pseudo-Nawbakhtī, *Firaq al-Shīʿa*, pp. 3–6. It is essentially confirmed by H. S. Nyberg in his article, 'Muʿtazila', *Shorter Encyclopaedia of Islam*. This postulation of a political origin of the Muʿtazila is more satisfactory than the usual theological explanation, and is supported by the fact that the Arabic verb *iʿtazala*, from which Muʿtazila is derived, means to be neutral (e.g. in Qurʾān, xliv, 20) or more specifically to be neutral in war. (See Lane, *Arabic-English Lexicon*, V, 2036.)
183. The Ibāḍiyya opposed the indiscriminate use of force and advocated resistance only against political leadership (Ashʿarī, *Maqālāt al-islāmiyyīn*, I, 189).
184. E.g., Kulīnī, *al-Uṣūl min al-Kāfī*, I, 334, 336.
185. See n. 179 above.
186. Resistance to the Fāṭimid claim of a divinely designated and omniscient – hence omnipotent – imām is admitted by none other than the famous Fāṭimid ideologue, al-Qāḍī al-Nuʿmān (d. 974). He expresses his impatience with the commoners for their insistence that the imāma is elective (*Daʿāʾim al-Islām*, I, 29–54) and that the guardians of religion are the community as a whole represented by the learned (ibid., I, 97–103).
187. Baghdādī (d. 1037) attributes to the extreme Shīʿīs the view that prophets are politicians who use laws as a device to achieve mastery over the commoners (*Uṣūl al-dīn*, p. 330).
188. Ghazzālī (d. 1111), in his attacks on extreme Shīʿīs (*Faḍāʾiḥ al-Bāṭiniyya*, p. 3), refers to their use of philosophy.
189. I find myself in disagreement with Professor Gibb's attribution of the eventual acceptance of political philosophy to Ṭūsī's (thirteenth-century) formulation that is contrasted with earlier Shīʿī-tinged theories ('Constitutional Organization', *Law in the Middle East*, ed. M. Khadduri and H. Liebesny, p. 25). First, Professor Gibb's extensive quote of Ṭūsī's formulation is a word for word reproduction of the tenth-century philosopher, Fārābī (*Fuṣūl al-madanī*, p. 137). Second, Ṭūsī was no less a Shīʿī than earlier philosophers. The supposed intellectual accommodation between political philosophy and traditionalism that E. I. J. Rosenthal

describes (*Political Thought in Medieval Islam*, pp. 214–5) is based on a mistaken reading of Ṭūsī's *'muḥdathān'* (modern philosophers) as *'muḥaddithān'* (traditionists)! The accommodation by Ṭūsī's time of philosophy to Orthodoxy is probably related not so much to an intellectual settlement as to the historical fact of the failure of the Ismā'īlī experiment with the disappearance of the Fāṭimid empire from the Muslim scene. One might still ask: 'Why was political philosophy accepted in the Ottoman empire in spite of the persistent use of Shī'ism as the banner of a rival, Safavid, empire?' A partial answer probably lies in the fact that the Safavids adopted not extreme Shī'ism but the moderate Twelver form which presented no internal threat to the Orthodox empire of the Ottomans.

190. H. S. Nyberg, 'Mu'tazila', *Shorter Encyclopaedia of Islam*, ed. H. A. R. Gibb and J. H. Kramers.
191. Early 'Abbāsid disputations on the imāma were mostly between Shī'īs and Mu'tazilites.
192. E.g., Jāḥiẓ, *'Uthmāniyya*, p. 261.
193. For an illustration of the contempt which some Mu'tazilites had for the common people, see ibid., pp. 250–79. Jāḥiẓ felt that politico-religious controversies are the province of a science just as specialized as medicine or astronomy, and, therefore, the commoners should not indulge in such controversies but should always defer to the elite who alone have the necessary specialization.
194. The Zaydīs, combining Mu'tazilism with Shī'ism, were willing to take greater chances (Ash'arī, *Maqālāt al-Islāmiyyīn*, II, 140).
195. For example, the famous theologian, Taftāzānī (d. 1390), writes: 'Obedience to the imām is obligatory whether he be just or unjust as long as he does not violate the ordinances of the Shar'' (Anon., *Sharḥ al-Maqāṣid*, II, 272).
196. Ibn al-Muqaffa', *al-Adab al-kabīr*, p. 85.
197. Fārābī, *Fuṣūl al-madanī*, p. 164.
198. Miskawayh, *Tahdhīb al-akhlāq*, p. 185.
199. E.g., Ṭabarī (d. 923) writes in his famous exegesis of the Qur'ān: 'Obedience is obligatory only to God, His Messenger or a just imām'. Ṭabarī goes on to say that God demands obedience to the rulers' commands that are in the public interest and that do not involve disobeying God (*Tafsīr al-Qur'ān*, VIII, 503).
200. Māwardī's older contemporary, Bāqillānī, states that according to 'many people' it is obligatory to depose an unjust imām (Tamhīd, p. 186). Another contemporary of Māwardī, Ibn Ḥazm, writes that – in addition to the Mu'tazila, the Khawārij and the Zaydiyya – 'certain segments of the Sunnīs' consider use of force against an unjust ruler a part of their duty to command good and prohibit evil (*al-Fiṣal fī al-milal wa al-niḥal*, IV, 132–5). The reluctance of some Sunni writers to deny the community the right of deposing an erring imām stems in part from the fact that this right was the stock Sunnī answer to the Shī'ī demand for an infallible imām. See, for example, Baghdādī (also a contemporary of Māwardī), *Uṣūl al-dīn*, p. 278.
201. Qur'ān, v, 104. Quoted, for example, in Abū Yūsuf, *Kitāb al-Kharāj*, p. 12.

202. Muslim, Ṣaḥīḥ, VI, 19–20.
203. Ibn Qutayba, *Ta'wīl mukhtalif al-ḥadīth*, p. 4.
204. Abū Yūsuf, *Kitāb al-Kharāj*, p. 11.
205. This hope for redress was embodied in the common saying: 'The most imminent of events is the fall of the oppressor, and the most penetrating of arrows is the prayer of the oppressed'.
206. Muslim, *Ṣaḥīḥ*, VI, 19.
207. This is the view, for example, of Māwardī's contemporary, the Hanbalite leader, Ibn al-Farrā' (*al-Mu'tamad*, fol. 76b).
208. Ibid., fol. 77b.
209. Māwardī, *Qawānīn*, p. 12.
210. Māwardī, *Siyāsa*, fol. 97b.
211. Ibid., fol. 16a.
212. Bīrūnī, *Āthār*, p. 132
213. Māwardī, *Aḥkām*, p. 31 (my italics).
214. I would agree with Professor Makdisi that the caliph was not too anxious to have the strong Saljūqs arrive in Baghad (George Makdisi, *Ibn 'Aqīl et la résurgence de l'Islam traditionaliste au XIe siècle*, pp. 78–103). But I would add two further considerations: first, the caliph did not have much choice in the matter, for he had little power to stop the steady westward march of the Saljūqs; second, he could easily have seen in the Saljūqs a lesser evil than the alliance of a military faction (e.g., under Basāsīri) with the Fātimid Caliphate – an alliance that would have threatened the very existence of the 'Abbāsid Caliphate.
215. Māwardī, *Aḥkām*, p. 56.
216. 'Al Mawardi's Theory of the Caliphate', *Studies on the Civilization of Islam*, ed. S. J. Shaw and W. R. Polk, pp. 150–65.
217. H. A. R. Gibb, 'Constitutional Organization', *Law in the Middle East*. ed. M. Khadduri and H. J. Liebesny, pp. 3–27.
218. Gibb, *Studies*, pp. 163–4.
219. Māwardī, *Tashīl*, fol. 32a.
220. Māwardī, *Siyāsa*, fol. 97a, b.
221. Ibid., fol. 60b.
222. Māwardī, *Tashīl*, fol. 61b.
223. Māwardī, *Siyāsa*, fol. 60b.
224. Māwardī, *Adab*, p. 328.
225. Ibid., p. 123.
226. No one English word conveys the full meaning of the word '*siyāsa*' which, as will be seen later, usually refers to government with the exception of the jurisdiction of the *qāḍī* (judge in accordance with Divine Law).
227. Subkī, *Mu'īd al-ni'am*, p. 41.
228. Taftāzānī, 'Maqāṣid', *Sharḥ al-Maqāṣid*, Anon., p. 272.
229. Subkī, *Mu'īd*, p. 34.
230. Ibid., p. 40.
231. Ibn Taymiyya, *al-Siyāsa al-shar'iyya*, especially p. 63. Like Ibn Taymiyya, most Muslim writers conceived of ideals not as goals to be reached but as points of reference towards which society is to strive. Ibn Taymiyya's contemporary, Ibn al-Ṭiqtaqā, thus misses the point when he expressed his impatience with the idealized picture of the first four caliphs – a picture that he deems fit for the

behaviour of prophets rather than kings (*al-Fakhrī fī al-ādāb al-sulṭāniyya*, p. 29).

232. The quotation from Ibn ʿAqīl's lost *Funūn* is reproduced in Ibn Qayyim, *al-Siyāsa al-sharʿiyya*, p. 15.
233. Ibid.
234. Ibn Qayyim, *al-Siyāsa al-sharʿiyya*, p. 16.
235. Ibid., p. 17.
236. Burhān al-Dīn al-Basnawī, *Risāla fī al-Siyāsa al-sharʿiyya*, MS 3037 of Yehuda Collection, fols 63b–66b.
237. Khayr al-Dīn, *Aqwam al-masālik*, p. 42.
238. Rashīd Riḍā, *al-Khilāfa*, p. 5.
239. Tabarī (d. 923), *Tafsīr al-Qur'ān*, VIII, 502; Zamakhsharī (d. 1144), *al-Kashshāf*, I, 405; Ibn al-Jawzī (d. 1200), *Zād al-masīr fī ʿilm al-tafsīr*, II, 116–17; al-Rāzī (d. 1209), *al-Tafsīr*, X, 143–6; Ibn al-ʿArabī (d. 1240), *Tafsīr*, I, 87, 153; Bayḍāwī (d. between 1282 and 1316), *Anwār al-tanzīl wa asrār al-ta'wīl*, II, 94–5; al-Ḥasan ibn ʿAbd Allah al-ʿAbbasi (wrote 1308), *Āthār al-uwal fī tadbīr al-duwal*, p. 29; Ibn Juzayy (d. 1340), *Kitāb al-tashīl li-ʿulūm al-tanzīl*, I, 146; Abū Ḥayyān al-Andalusī (d. 1345), *al-Baḥr al-muḥīṭ*, III, 278; al-Fayrūzabādī (d. 1415), *Tanwīr al-miqbās min tafsīr Ibn ʿAbbās*, p. 48; Ibn Ḥajar al-ʿAsqalānī (d. 1448), *Fatḥ al-bārī bi-sharḥ al-Bukhārī*, XVI, 226; al-ʿAynī (d. 1451), *ʿUmdat al-Qārī fī Sharḥ Ṣaḥīḥ al-Bukhārī*, XXIII, 221; al-Suyūṭī (d. 1505), *al-Durr al-manthūr fī al-tafsīr bil-ma'thūr*, II, 176; al-Qastalāni (d. 1517), *Irshād al-sārī li-sharḥ Ṣaḥīḥ al-Bukhārī*, p. 216; Muḥammad Rashīd Riḍā (d. 1935), *Tafsīr al-manār*, V, 181; Darwaza (still living), *al-Tafsīr al-ḥadīth*, IX, 104.
240. Qur'ān, iv, 59.
241. Anonymous, *Najāt al-umma fī ṭāʿat al-a'imma*, in Yehuda MS 4275, fols 26b–27a.
242. It is natural that the *ʿulamā'* put religion before justice. They usually held that the ruler's duties to defend and spread the Faith and to expand Muslim power demand that he be a Muslim. Thus they mostly rejected – a few accepting with reluctance – the argument of Mongol conquerors (Ibn al-Ṭiqṭaqā, *al-Fakhrī*, p. 17) or Western imperialists that the just rule of an infidel who did not interfere with the *sharīʿa* (i.e., the *ʿulamā'*) was preferable to the oppressive rule of a Muslim.
243. Such perplexity is attested to by Nawawī (d. 1278) as quoted by Bahā' al-Kuwwa, *al-Manāhij al-mubāriziyya* (in MS 4141 of Yehuda Collection, fol. 31a).
244. E.g., Ibn Ḥajar al-ʿAsqalānī, *Fatḥ al-bārī*, XVI, 241.
245. E.g., Ibn Bājja (d. 1138), *Tadbīr al-mutawaḥḥid*.
246. E.g., Shahrastānī, *Nihāyat al-iqdām fī ʿilm al-kalām*, p. 496.
247. Ibn Ḥazm, *al-Fiṣal fī al-milal wa al-niḥal*, pp. 132–5.
248. Juwaynī expresses his position in the following words: 'When the ruler of the time becomes oppressive and his injustice and repression become evident, then those who loosen and bind have the right, if words fail to turn him away from his evil deeds, to plot his removal even should this involve the use of force and the waging of war' (*al-Irshād*, p. 370).
249. Ghazzālī's position (*Iḥyā'*, p. 343) differs from Māwardī's only in

emphasis. Both were against any course of action that would lead to sedition. But Ghazzālī seems to be more pessimistic about the possibilities of using force against an unjust ruler without producing sedition.

250. See, for example: Ṭabarī, *Tafsīr*, VII, 90–1; Zamakhsharī, *Kashshāf*, I, 304; Ibn al-Jawzī, *Zād al-masīr*, I, 434–5; Ibn al-'Arabī, *Tafsīr*, I, 123; Bayḍāwī, *Anwār al-tanzīl*, II, 35; Fayrūzabādī, *Tanwîr al-miqbās*, p. 43; Suyūṭī, *al-Durr al-manthūr*, II, 62.
251. Abū Ḥayyān al-Andalusī, *al-Baḥr al-muḥīṭ*, III, 20–1.
252. E.g., Ījī, *al-Mawāqif*, VIII, 353.
253. E.g., Nasafī, *'Aqā'd*, in Taftāzānī, *Sharḥ*, p. 72; Taftāzānī, *Maqāṣid*, in Anonymous, *Sharḥ*, II, 274–5.
254. For a new light on the growth of educational institutions, see George Makdisi, 'Muslim Institutions of Learning in Eleventh Century Baghdād', *Bulletin of the School of Oriental and African Studies*, XXIV (1961), pp. 1–56.
255. See Paul Wittek, *The Rise of the Ottoman Empire.*
256. Naqshabandī, *Hidāyat al-ḥunafā' ilā ṭā'at al-khulafā'*, fol. 29a, b.
257. E.g., Khayr al-Dīn al-Tūnīsī (d. 1890), *Aqwam al-masālik fī ma'rifat aḥwāl al-mamālik*, pp. 4–50, especially 8, 11, 12, 13, 41, 42.
258. E g., Aḥmad Shakīr in his edition of Ibn al-Jawzī, *Zād al-masīr*, I, 486, n. 2.
259. E.g., Aḥmad Shakīr (ibid.) attacks vehemently those Muslims who, imitating the modern West, would give the people the right of legislation. Similarly, the Secretary-General of 'The Society of North African *'Ulamā'*' (Kannūn, 'Al-amr bil ma'rūf wa al-nahy 'an al-munkar', *Majallat al-Azhar* (1964), pp. 80–4) expresses outrage at those who would refer matters that involve the interest of the Community to the fallible 'people' rather than to the infallible Qur'ān and Sunna (i.e., *'ulamā'*).
260. Ibn Khaldūn (d. 1406), though not a thoroughgoing empiricist, stands out for his utilization of an empirical approach. See M. Mahdi, *Ibn Khaldūn's Philosophy of History.*
261. A notable exception in Islam is the minor but important current of classical political philosophy.
262. *Al-manhaj al-maslūk fī siyāsat al-mulūk*, pp. 22–3. While the published edition of the book gives the name of the author as 'Abd al-Raḥmān ibn 'Abd Allāh, Brockelmann, basing his description on a number of manuscripts, is probably more correct in giving the name of the author as 'Abd al-Raḥmān ibn Naṣr al-Shayzarī.
263. *Ma'ālim al-qurbā fi aḥkām al-ḥisba*, chs I, II.
264. *Muqaddima*, Book I, ch. 34, p. 236.
265. *Ṣubḥ al-a'shā fī ṣinā'at al-inshā*, II, 5.
266. *Miftāḥ al-sa'āda*, I, 345.
267. L. Ostrorg, *Les constitutions politique* – incomplete; F. Fagnan, *Les statuts governmentaux*; S. Keijzer, *Māwardī's publick en administratief regt van den Islam*; H. F. Amendroz, *Journal of the Royal Asiatic Society*, 1910, 1911, 1916.
268. *Aqwam al-masālik fī ma'rifat al-mamālik*, p. 15.
269. *al-Khilāfa.*
270. See, for example, Diyā'al-Dīn al-Rayyis, *al-Naẓarāt al-siyāsiyya fī al-Islām.*

271. Ibn al-Jawzī, *Muntaẓam*, VIII, 26.
272. Ibid., VII, 270; VIII, 26.
273. Shīrāzī, *Ṭabaqāt al-fuqahā'*, p. 110.
274. Subkī, *Ṭabaqāt*, II, 233; Ibn al-'Imād, *Shadharāt*, III, 152.
275. Shīrāzī, *Ṭabaqāt al-fuqahā'*, p. 110.
276. Baghdādī, *Ta'rīkh Baghdād*, XII, 102.
277. Shīrāzī, op. cit., p. 110.
278. Subkī, op. cit., III, 31, 41, 223, 237, 249, 284, 298, 303; IV, 42.
279. Ibn al-Jawzī, op. cit., VII, 143; Ibn al-Athīr, *Kāmil*, IX, 384.
280. Yaqūt, *Irshād*, V, 407.
281. Ibn al-Athīr, op. cit., IX, 284–5.
282. Ibn al-Jawzī, op. cit., VIII, 65.
283. Ibid., p. 89.
284. Ibn al-Athīr, op. cit., IV, 309.
285. Ibn al-Jawzī, op. cit., VIII, 97; Ibn al-Athīr, op. cit., IX, 312–13; Subkī, op. cit., III, 305.
286. Yaqūt, op. cit., V, 407.
287. Ibn al-Jawzī, op. cit., VIII, 113–14; Ibn al-Athīr, op. cit., IX, 350.
288. Ibn al-Jawzī, op. cit., VIII, 116; Ibn al-Athīr, op. cit., IX, 357.
289. Mentioned by: Suyūṭī, *Itqān*, II, 131; Ṭāshköprüzāde, *Miftāḥ*, II, 368; Hājjī Khalīfa, *Kashf*, I, 168.
290. Yāqut, op. cit., V, 407.
291. Ibid., V, 407. [Yet a small manuscript with this title related to Māwardī was found. Khidr Muhammad Khidr published it in Kuwait.]
292. Baghdādī, op. cit., XII, 102; Shīrāzī, op. cit., 110; Sam'ānī, *Ansāb*, p. 504; Ibn al-Jawzī, op. cit., VIII, 199; Ibn Khallikān, *Wafayāt*, II, 444.
293. Māwardī, *A'lām*, p. 158.
294. Sakhāwī, *I'lān*, p. 91.
295. Brockelmann, *Geschichte der Arabischen Litteratur*, I, 483; Supplement I, 668.
296. Ibn al-Jawzī's substitution of 'al-Muqtaran' for 'al-'uyūn' (*Muntẓam*, VIII, 199) and Yāfi'ī's substitution of 'al-Qalb' for 'al-Nukat' (*Mir'āt al-janān*, III, 72) are obviously copying errors. [Māwardī's book of exegesis was published in Kuwait, critically edited by Khidr Muhammad Khidr in four volumes. But some scholars suggest that what we have is an abridgement of Māwardī's commentary, by Izz el-Din Ibn Abd el-Salam in the seventh century of the Hegira.]
297. Ibn Khallikān, op. cit., II, 444; Abū al-Fidā', *Mukhtaṣar*, II, 179; Yāfi'ī, op. cit., III, 72; Hājjī Khalīfa, op. cit., I, 458; II, 1978.
298. F. Sayyid, 'Makhṭūṭāt al-Yaman', *Majallat ma'had al-makhṭūṭāt al-'arabiyya*, I, 201.
299. Leon Nemoy, *Arabic Manuscripts in the Yale University Library* ('Transactions of the Conneticut Academy of Arts and Sciences', Vol. 40).
300. Subkī, op. cit., III, 174.
301. Māwardī, *al-Ḥāwī*, I, fol. 1. [*Al-Ḥāwī* was published as a whole in 1993 by Dar al-Kutub al-Ilmiyya, Beirut. It seems that Mukhtasar al-Muzani was the basis of arranging the book. But *al-Ḥāwī* was enlarged too much, and that led to considerable departures from its model.]

302. Subkī, op. cit., III, 303; Tāshköprüzāde, op. cit., II, 190.
303. Ibn al-Jawzī, op. cit., VIII, 199. [*Al-Amthāl wa al-ḥikam* was critically edited and published by Fu'ād Abd al-Mun'im Ahmad.]
304. Yāqūt, op. cit., V, 407.
305. For a description of this manuscript, *al-Aḥkām fī al-ḥisba al-sharīfa*, see the article by Aḥmad Sāmiḥ al-Khālidī in *al-Thaqāfa*, VII, 47. Although he noticed the identity of this manuscript with Ibn al-Ukhuwwa's work, Mr Khālidī was inclined to attribute the work to Māwardī.
306. *Al-Rutba fī ṭalab al-ḥisba*, Fātih 3495.
307. Ibn al-Ukhuwwa, *Ma'ālim al-qurbā fī aḥkām al-hisba.*
308. A parallel conclusion was reached by Monsieur Gaudefroy-Demombynes, 'Sur quelques ouvrages de *ḥisba*', *Journal Asiatique* 230 (1938), pp. 449–57.
309. Shayzarī, *Nihāyat al-rutba fī ṭalab al-ḥisba.*
310. Bibliothèque Nationale, Paris.
311. Subkī, *Mu'īd al-ni'am.*
312. See, for example, his excessive praise of the Mu'tazilite caliphs.
313. Māwardī's relationship to the Mu'tazilites has been dealt with in earlier sections.
314. Māwardī, *Naṣīḥa*, fol. 14.
315. Tha'ālibī, *Yatīma*, I, 124.
316. Ibn Taghribirdī, *Nujūm*, IV, 139.
317. Māwardī, *Naṣīḥa*, fol. 20.
318. Māwardī, *Adab al-dunyā wa al-dīn*, p. 196.
319. In his introduction to *Aḥkam*, Enger gives a quotation (p. iv) indicating that Māwardī was reading his book *Adab al-dunyā wa al-dīn* to a group in the mosque at Wāsiṭ in AH 421. *Tashīl* must have been written after AH 428, for Māwardī speaks of his mission between two kings (*Tashīl*, fol. 37), a clear reference to his mediation between Abū Kālījār and Jalāl al-Dawla in AH 428 (see biographical note above).
320 Ibn al-Jawzī, op. cit., VII, 199; Yāqūt, op. cit., V, 407; Abū al-Fidā', *Mukhtaṣar*, II, 179; Ibn Taghribirdī, op. cit., II, 234.
321. Ḥājjī Khalīfa, op. cit., II, 1011.
322. Ziriklī, *A'lām*, V, 147–8; Baghdādī, *Hidyat al-'ārifīn*, p. 1,689.
323. Ibn Khallikān, op. cit., II, 444.
324. Ṭāshköprüzāde, op. cit., II, 190.
325. R. Enger (*De Vita et Scriptis Maverdii*) assumed that the Paris manuscript was a translation of Ghazzālī's *Naṣīḥat al-mulūk* (written in Persian). This is definitely not the case.
326. Māwardī, *Naṣīḥa*, fol. 4.

Selected Bibliography

Only works that are referred to in the text or notes are listed. An asterisk before an entry indicates a manuscript. The date given for earlier authors is the AD date of death unless otherwise indicated. If the lunar year falls in two solar years, only the first AD year is given. An incorrect title or author is indicated by quotation marks with correct listing following in parentheses.

fl. 1308 al-ʿAbbāsī, al-Hasan ibn ʿAbd Allāh. *Āthar al-uwal fī tartīb al-duwal.* Cairo, AH 1295 (AD 1878).

1331 Abū al-Fidā', Ismā'īl ibn ʿAlī. *al-Mukhtaṣar fī akhbār al-bashar.* Cairo: al-Matbaʿa al-Husayniyya al-Miṣriyya, AH 1325 (AD 1907).

1345 Abū Hayyān al-Andalusī. *al-Baḥr al-muḥīt.* Cairo: Maṭbaʿat al-Saʿāda, AH 1328 (AD 1910).

1095 Abū Shujāʿ al-Rudhrāwarī, Muḥammad ibn al-Ḥusayn. *Dhayl Kitāb tajārib al-umam.* Edited by H. F. Amedroz in Vol. III of the *Eclipse of the Abbasid Caliphate.* Cairo: Matbaʿat Sharikat al-Tamaddun al-Ṣināʿiyya, AH 1334 (AD 1916).

1066 Abū Yaʿlā ibn al-Farrā', Muḥammad ibn al-Ḥusayn. *al-Aḥkām al-sulṭāniyya.* Edited by Muḥammad Hāmid al-Faqī. Cairo: Muṣṭafā Bābī al-Ḥalabī, AH 1356 (AD 1938).

* —. *al-Muʿtamad fī uṣūl al-dīn.* Damascus: Ẓāhiriyya, MS No. 45.

798 Abū Yūsuf Yaʿqūb ibn Ibrāhīm. *Kitāb al-Kharāj.* Cairo: al-Maṭbaʿa al-Salafiyya, AH 1346 (AD 1927).

c. 942 Āhmad ibn Yūsuf ibn Ibrāhīm, 'al-ʿUhūd al-Yūnāniyya', Uṣūl. Edited by Badawī.

Amedroz, H. F. 'The Hisba Jurisdiction in the Aḥkām Sulṭāniyya of Māwardī', *Journal of the Royal Asiatic Society*, 1916.

—. 'The Maẓālim Jurisdiction in the Aḥkām Sulṭāniyya of Mawardī', *Journal of the Royal Asiatic Society*, 1911.

—. 'The Office of Kāḍī in the Aḥkām Sulṭāniyya of Mawardī', *Journal of the Royal Asiatic Society*, 1910.

992 al-ʿĀmirī, Abū al-Ḥasan Muḥammad. *al-Saʿāda wa al-isʿād.* Wiesbaden: University of Tehran Publication No. 435, 1957–8.

al-ʿAmirī. Also see Rosenthal, F.

Arberry, A. J., *Revelation and Reason in Islam.* London: George Allen & Unwin Ltd., 1957.

al-Arzanjānī Uways Wafā'. *Minhāj al-yaqīn*, Sharḥ *Adab al-dunyā wa al-din.* Istanbul, AH 1328 (AD 1903).

935 al-Ashʿarī, Abū al-Ḥasan ʿAlī. *al-Ibāna ʿan uṣūl al-diyāna.* Hyderabad, AH 1321 (AD 1903).

—. *Maqālāt al-islamiyyīn.* Cairo: Maktabat al-Nahḍa, 1950.

Averroes. See Ibn Rushd.

Avicenna. See Ibn Sīnā.

1451 al-ʿAynī, Badr al-dīn Abū Muḥammad Maḥmūd ibn Aḥmad. *ʿUmdat al-qārī fī sharḥ Ṣaḥīḥ al-Bukhārī*. Cairo: Idārat al-Ṭibāʿa al-Munīriyya, n.d.

Badawī, ʿAbd al-Raḥmān (ed.). *al-Uṣūl al-yūnāniyya lil-naẓarāt al-siyāsiyya fī al-Islām*. Vol. I. Cairo: Maktabat al-Nahḍa al-Miṣriyya, 1954.

1037 al-Baghdādī, Abū Manṣūr ʿabd al-Qāhir ibn Ṭāhir. *al-Farq bayn al-firaq*. Edited by Muḥammad Badr. Cairo: Maṭbaʿat.

—. *Uṣūl al-dīn*. Istanbul: Maṭbaʿat al-Dawla, 1928.

al-Baghdādī, Ismāʿīl. *Hidyat al-ʿārifīn*. Istanbul. 1951.

c. 1353 *Bahā' al-Kuwwa, ʿUthmān ibn ʿAlī. *al-Manāhij al-mubāriziyya*. Princeton, Yehuda Collection, in MS No. 414.

1013 al-Bāqillānī, Abū Bakr Muḥammad. *al-Tamhīd fī al-radd ʿalā al-mulḥida* etc. Edited by Maḥmūd al-Khuḍayrī and Muḥammad Abū Rīda. Cairo: Dār al-fikr al-ʿArabī, AH 1366 (AD 1947).

1565 *al-Basnawī, Burhān al-Dīn ibn Ibrāhīm. *Risālā fī al-siyāsa al-sharʿiyya*. Princeton, Yehuda Collection, in MS No. 3037.

c. 1300 al-Bayḍāwī, ʿAbd Allāh ibn ʿUmar. *Tafsīr* [*al Qur'ān* or *Anwār al-tanzil wa asrār al-ta'wīl*]. Cairo: al-Maktaba al-Tijāriyya, n.d.

1048 Bīrūnī, Muḥammad ibn Aḥmad. *al-Āthār al-bāqiya ʿan al-qurūn al-khāliya*. Edited by C. E. Sachau. Leipzig, 1878.

Brockelmann, Carl. *Geschichte der Arabischen Litteratur*. Leiden: Brill, 1937–42 (Supplementary Vols I, II, III), 1943–9 (2nd edn, Vols I, II).

Cahen, Claude, ed. *L'elaboration de l'Islam*. Paris: Presses universitaires de France, 1961.

Canard, M. 'Bagdād au IVe siècle de l'hégire (Xe siècle de l'ère chrétienne)'. *Arabica*, Vol. spécial (1963), 269–89.

Darwaza, Muḥammad ʿIzzat. *al-Tafsīr al-Ḥadīth*. Cairo: Dār Iḥyā' al-Kutub al-ʿArabiyya, 1963.

The Encyclopaedia of Islam. Leiden: Brill, 1913–24 (lst edn), 1938 (supplement), 1960 (2nd edn).

Enger, R. *De Vita et Scriptis Maverdii*. Bonn 1851.

950 al-Fārābī, Abū Naṣr Muḥammad. *Fuṣūl al-madanī*. Edited and translated by D. M. Dunlop. Cambridge: University Press, 1961.

—. *Iḥṣā'al-ʿulūm*. Cairo: Dār al-fikr al-ʿArabī, 1949.

—. *al-Jamʿbayna ra'y al-ḥakīmayn*. Edited by Albert Nader. Beirut: Catholic Press, 1959.

1415 al-Fayrūzabādī, Abū Ṭāhir Muḥammad ibn Yaʿqūb. *Tanwīr al-miqbās min Tafsīr ibn ʿAbbās*. Cairo: Muṣṭafā Babī al-Halabī, 1951.

Gardet, Louis. *La Cité Musulmane*. Paris: Librairie Philosophique, 1954.

Gaudefroy-Demombynes, M. 'Sur quelques ouvrages de hisba', *Journal Asiatique*, Vol. 230 (1938).

1111 al-Ghazzālī, Abū Ḥamid Muḥammad. *Faḍā'iḥ al-Bāṭiniyya*. Edited by I. Goldziher. Leyden: Brill, 1916.

—. *Iḥyā' ʿulūm al-dīn*. Cairo: al-Maktaba al-Tijāriyya, n.d.

—. *al-Tibr al-masbūk fī naṣīḥat al-mulūk*. Cairo: Maṭbaʿat al-Adāb wa al-Mu'ayyad, AH 1317 (AD 1899).
Gibb, H. A. R. 'Constitutional Organization', *Law in the Middle East*. Edited by M. Khadduri and H. J. Liebesny. Washington: The Middle East Institute, 1955.
—. 'Government and Islam under the Early Abbasid', *L'elaboration de l'Islam*. Edited by Claude Cahen. Paris: Presses Universitaires de France, 1961.
—. 'Al-Māwardi's Theory of the Caliphate', *Studies on the Civilization of Islam*. Edited by W. R. Polk and S. J. Shaw. Boston: Beacon Press, 1962.
—. 'Some Considerations on the Sunni Theory of the Caliphate', *Studies on the Civilization of Islam*. Edited by W. R. Polk and S. J. Shaw. Boston: Beacon Press, 1962.
Gilson, Etienne. *Reason and Revelation in the Middle Ages*. New York: C. Scribner's Sons, 1938.
Grunebaum, G. E. von. *Medieval Islam*. 2nd edition Chicago: University of Chicago Press, 1953.
—, ed. *Unity and Variety in Muslim Civilization*. Chicago: University of Chicago Press, 1955.
1657 Hājjī Khalīfa, Muṣṭafā ibn ʿAbd Allāh. *Kashf al-ẓunūn ʿan asāmī al-kutub wa al-funūn*. London, 1835–58.
al-Ḥusaynī Abū Bakr ibn Hidāyat Allāh. Ṭabaqāt al-shāfiʿiyyā. Baghdad, AH 1356 (AD 1937).
940 Ibn ʿAbd Rabbih, Aḥmad. *al-ʿIqd al-farīd*. Edited by Aḥmad Amīn et al. Cairo: Lajnat al-Ta'līf wa al-Tarjama wa al-Nashr, 1940.
fl. 840 Ibn Abī al-Rabīʿ, Aḥmad ibn Muḥammad. Sulūk al-mālik fī tadbīr al-mamālik. Cairo, AH 1286 (AD 1869).
Ibn al-Ahwāzī, Abū al-Ḥasan ʿAlī. *al-Tibr al-munsabik fī tadbīr al-malik*. Cairo: Maṭbaʿat al-Tamaddun, AH 1318 (AD 1900).
1240 Ibn al-ʿArabī, Muḥammad ibn ʿAlī. *Tafsīr*. Cairo, n.d.
1176 Ibn ʿAsākir, Abū al-Qāsim ʿAlī. *Tabyīn kadhib al-muftarī fīma nusiba ilā al-imām Abī al-Ḥasan al-Ashʿarī*. Damascus: al-Qudsī, AH 1347 (AD 1927).
1234 Ibn al-Athīr, 'Izz al-Dīn ʿAlī ibn Muḥammad. *al-Kāmil fī al-ta'rikh*. Edited by A. J. Tornberg. Leiden: Brill, 1851–83 AD.
1138 Ibn Bājja, Abū Bakr Muḥammad ibn Yaḥyā. *Tadbīr al-mutawaḥḥid*. Edited and translated (into Spanish) by Don Miguel Asín Palacios, Madrid-Granada, 1946.
997 Ibn Baṭṭa al-ʿUkbarī. *Kitāb al-Sharḥ wa al-ibāna ʿalā uṣūl al-sunna wa al-diyāna*. Edited and translated by H. Laoust. Damascus: French Institute, 1958.
c. 827 Ibn al-Birtīq, Yaḥyā. 'Sirr al-Asrār', *Uṣūl*. Edited by Badawī.
Ibn al-Farrā'. See Abū Yaʿlā ibn al-Farrā'.
1448 Ibn Ḥajar al-ʿAsqalānī, Abū al-Faḍl Aḥmad. *Fatḥ al-bārī bi-sharḥ al-Bukhārī*. Cairo: Muṣṭafā Babī al-Ḥalabī, 1959.
—. *Lisān al-mīzān*. Hyderabad: Mathaʿat Majlis Dā'irat al-Maʿārif al-Niẓāmiyya, AH 1329–31 (AD 1911–13).
1064 Ibn Ḥazm, Abū Muḥammad ʿAlī ibn Aḥmad. *al-fiṣal fī al-milal wa al-niḥal*. Cairo, AH 1347 (AD 1928).
1678 Ibn al-ʿImād, Abū al-Falāh ʿAbd al-Ḥayy. *Shadharāt al-dhahab*

fī akhbār man dhahab. Cairo: Maktabt al-Qudsī. AH 1350–1 (AD 1931–2).
1333 Ibn Jamā'a, 'Tahrīr al-Ahkām', *Islamica* VI. Edited by H. Kofler. Leipzig, 1934.
1200 Ibn al-Jawzī, Abū al-Faraj 'Abd al-Raḥmān. *al-Muntaẓam fī ta'rīkh al-mulūk wa al-umam*. Hyderabad: Matba'at dā'irat al-Ma'ārif al-'Uthmāniyya, AH 1357–9 (AD 1939–41).
—. *Zād al-masīr fī 'ilm al-tafsīr*. Damascus: al-Maktab al-islāmī lil-Ṭibā'a wa al-Nashr, 1964.
1340 Ibn Juzayy, Muḥammad ibn Aḥmad. *Kitāb al-tashīl li-'ulūm al-tanzīl*. Cairo: al-Maktaba al-Tijāriyya, AH 1355 (AD 1936).
1373 *Ibn Kathīr, 'Imād al-Dīn Abū al-fīdā' Ismā'īl. *Tabaqāt al-shāfī'iyya*. Manuscript in Princeton University Collection, not catalogued.
1406 Ibn Khaldūn, 'Abd al-Raḥmān. *al-Muqaddima*. Beirut: al-Ma'tba'a al-Adabiyya, 1900.
1281 Ibn Khallikān, Aḥmad. *Wafayāt al a'yan wa anbā' abnā' al-zaman*. Edited by Muḥammad 'Abd al-Ḥamīd. Cairo: Maktabat al-Nahḍa, 1948–9.
759 Ibn al-Muqaffa', 'Abd Allāh. *al-Adab al-ṣaghīr, al-Adab al-kabīr* and *Risālat al-ṣahāba*. Beirut: Maktabat al-Bayān, 1960.
1437 Ibn al-Murtaḍā, Aḥmad ibn Yaḥyā. *al-Mu'tazila* (extract of *Kitāb al-munya wa al-amal fī sharḥ kitāb al-milal wa al-niḥal*). Edited by T. W. Arnold. Leipzig, 1902.
995 Ibn al-Nadīm, Abū al-Faraj Muḥammad ibn Isḥāq. *al-Fīhrist*. Cairo, n.d.
1356 Ibn Qayyim al-Jawziyya, Abū 'Abd Allāh Muḥammad ibn Abī Bakr. *al-Ṭurq al-ḥukmiyya fī al-siyāsa al-shar'iyya*. Cairo: al-Mu'assasa al-'Arabiyya lil-Ṭibā'a wa al-Nashr, 1961.
889 Ibn Qutayba, Abū Muḥammad 'Abd Allāh. *Ta'wīl mukhtalif al-ḥadīth*. Cairo, AH 1326 (AD 1908).
—. *'Uyūn al-akhbār*. Cairo: Dar al-Kutub al-Miṣriyya, AH 1343 (AD 1925).
1189 Ibn Rushd, Abū al-Walīd Muḥammad. *Kitāb faṣl al-maqāl wa taqrīr mā bayn al-sharī'a wa al-ḥikma min al-ittiṣāl*. Edited by George Hourani. Leiden: Brill, 1959.
1037 Ibn Sīnā, Abū 'Alī al-Ḥusayn. 'al-Ilāhiyyāt', *al-Shifā'*. Vol. II. Cairo: al-Hay'a al-'Āmma li-Shu'ūn al-Maṭābi' al-Amīriyya, 1960.
1469 Ibn Taghrībirdī, Abū al-Maḥāsin Yūsuf. *al-Nujūm al-zāhira fī mulūk miṣr wa al-Qāhira*. Edited by William Popper. Berkeley: The University Press, 1909–30.
1328 Ibn Taymiyya, Taqī al-Dīn Aḥmad. *al-Siyāsa al-shar'iyya fī islāh al-rā'ī wa al-ra'iyya*. Cairo: al Maṭba'a al-Khayriyya, AH 1322 (AD 1904).
fl. 1301 Ibn al-Ṭiqtaqā, Muḥammad ibn 'Alī ibn Ṭabāṭabā. *al-Fakhrī fī al-ādāb al-sulṭāniyya wa al-duwal al-islāmiyya*. Beirut: Sādir, 1960.
1330 Ibn al-Ukhuwwa Ḍiyā' al-Dīn Muḥammad. *Ma'ālim al-qurbā fī aḥkām al-ḥisba*. Edited by Reuben Levy, Cambridge: University Press, 1938.

1352 Ibn Ziyān, Mūsā ibn Yūsuf. *Wāsiṭat al-sulūk fī siyāsat al-mulūk*. Tunis: Maṭba'at al-Dawla, AH 1279 (AD 1862).

1446 al-Ibshīhī, Shihāb al-Dīn Aḥmad. *al-Mustaṭraf fī kull fann mustaẓraf*. Cairo, AH 1277 (AD 1860).

1355 al-Ijī, 'Aḍud al-Dīn 'Abd al-Raḥmān. *al-Mawāqif*. Sharḥ al-Jurjānī. Cairo: Maṭba'at al-Sa'āda, 1907.

by 984 Ikhwān al-Safā'. *Rasāil*. 4 vols. Edited by Khayr al-dīn al-Ziriklī. Cairo: al-Maṭb'a al-'Arabiyya, 1928.

1108 al-Ishbīlī, Abū Bakr ibn Khayr. *Fihrist* (mā rawh 'an shuyūkhih). Zaragoza, 1893.

c. 883 [Pseudo-] Jāḥiẓ, Abū 'Uthmān 'Amr ibn Baḥr. *Kitāb al-Tāj fī akhlāq al-mulūk*. Beirut: Dar al-Fikr, 1955.

868 al-Jāḥiẓ, 'Amr ibn Baḥr. *al-'Uthmāniyya*. Edited by M. Hārūn. Cairo, 1955.

1085 *al-Juwaynī, 'Abd al-Malik ibn 'Abd Allāh ibn Yūsuf. *Ghiyāth al-umam fī iltiyāth al-ẓulam*. Alexandria: al-Baladiyya MS No. 1749B.

—. *Kitāb al-irshād ilā qawāti' al-adilla fī uṣūl al-i'tiqād*. Cairo: al-Khānjī, 1950.

1069 Kai Ka'ūs ibn Iskander. *Qābūs Nāma*. Translated by Reuben Levy. London: Cresset Press, 1951.

Kannūn, 'Abd Allāh. 'al-Amr bil-Ma'rūf wa al-nahy 'an al-munkan', *Majallat al-Azhar* (January 1964).

Khadduri, M. and H. J. Liebesny (eds). *Law in the Middle East*. Washington: The Middle East Institute, 1955.

al-Khālidī, Aḥmad Sāmiḥ. 'Hawla kitāb fī al-hisba, hal intaḥala Ibn al-Ukhuwwa kitāb al-Māwardī?', *al-Thaqāfa* (Cairo), Vol VII (1939).

1070 al-Khaṭīb al-Baghdādī, Abū Bakr Aḥmad. *Ta'rikh Baghdād*. Cairo: al-Khānjī, 1931.

1890 Khayr al-Dīn al-Tunisī. *Aqwam al-masālik fī ma'rifat aḥwāl al-mamālik*. Tunis: Maṭba'at al-Dawla, 1867.

al-Khuwarizmi. See al-Khwārizmi.

993 al-Khwārizmi, Abū 'Abd Allāh Muḥammad ibn Aḥmad. *Mafātīḥ al-'ulūm*. Edited by G. Van Vloten. Leiden, 1895.

870 al-Kindī, Ya'qūb ibn Isḥāq. 'Fī al-falsafa al-ūlā', *Rasā'il al-Kindī al-falsafiyya*. 2 vols. Edited by Abū Rīda. Cairo, 1950–3.

939 al-Kulīnī, Abū Ja'far Muḥammad ibn Ya'qūb. *al-Uṣūl min al-Kāfī*. Edited by 'Alī Akbar al-Shaffārī. Tehran: Maktabat al-Ṣaqūq, AH 1381 (AD 1961).

Lambton, A. D. S. 'Justice in the medieval Persian theory of kingship', *Studia Islamica*, Vol. XVII, 1962.

c. 1032 al-Maghribī, Abū al-Qāsim al-Ḥusayn ibn 'Alī. *Kitāb fī al-Siyāsa*. Edited by Sāmī al-Dahhān. Damascus: al-Ma'had al-Faransī lil-Dirāsāt al-'Arabiyya, AH 1367 (AD 1948).

Mahdi, Muhsin. *Ibn Khaldūn's Philosophy of History*. The University of Chicago Press, Phoenix Edition, 1964.

Makdisi, George. 'Ash'arī and the Ash'arites in Islamic Religious History', *Studia Islamica*, Vol. XVII, 1962.

—. *Ibn 'Aqīl et le Résurgence de l'Islam traditionaliste au XIe siècle*. Damascus: French Institute, 1963.

—. 'Muslim Institutions of Learning in Eleventh-Century

Baghdād', *Bulletin of the School of Oriental and African Studies*, XXIV (1961).

1058 al-Māwardī, Abū al-Ḥasan 'Alī. *Adab al-dunyā wa al-dīn*. Edited by Muṣṭafā al-saqqā'. Cairo: Muṣṭafā Bābī al-Ḥalabī and Sons, 1955. (German translation: Das Kitab 'Adab eddunjâ wa'ddîn', Oscar Rescher. Stuttgart, 1932–3.)

—. *'Adab al-qāḍī'*. (In fact a Vol. of *al-Ḥāwī*.) Istanbul: Suleymeniye, MS No. 381. (MSS of other volumes are at Princeton and Yale University libraries.)

—. *'Adab al-wazīr* al-ma'rūf bi *Qawānīn al-wizāra wa siyāsat al-mulk'*. (Correct title is *Qawānīn al-wizāra*.) Cairo: al-Khānjī, 1929. (Also Arabic MS No. 1528 at Yale University Library.)

—. *al-Aḥkām al-sulṭāniyya*. Edited by M. Enger. Bonn, 1853. (French translations: *Les status gouvernementaux ou règles de droit public et administratif*, by E. Fagnan. Alger: Jourdan, 1915. *Traité de droit public musulman*, by Leon Ostrorg. Paris, 1901 [incomplete].)

—. *A'lām al-nubuwwa*. Cairo: Matba'at Sharikat al-Tamaddun al-Sinā'iyya, AH 1330 (AD 1911).

*—. *al-Amthāl wa al-ḥikam*. Leiden: Bibliotheek der Rijksuniversiteit, Arabic MS No. 382.

*—. *al-Ḥāwī fī furū' al-fiqh*. Cairo: Dār al-kutub, Fiqh Shāfi'ī, MS 164.

*—. *'Naṣīhat al-mulūk'*. (Correct title is *Siyāsat al-mulk*.) Paris: Bibliotheque Nationale, Arabic MS No. 24473.

—. *Qawānīn al-wizāra*. See *Adab al-wazīr*.

*'—'. *al-Rutba fī ṭalab al-ḥisba*. Istanbul: Fātiḥ, MS No. 3495. (Actual author is Ibn al-Ukhuwwa; al-Māwardī is the author of the first two chapters only.)

*—. *Siyāsat al-mulk*. See *Naṣīḥat al-mulūk*.

*—. *Tafsīr al-Qur'ān*. Princeton University Library, Garrett Collection, MS No. 1258.

*—. *Tashīl al-naẓar wa ta'jīl al-ẓafar*. Gotha: Landesbibliothek, Arabic MS No. 1872.

1030 Miskawayh, Aḥmad ibn Muḥammad. *Risāla fī māhiyyat al-'adl*. Edited by M. S. Khan. Leiden: Brill, 1964.

—. *Tahdhīb al-akhlāq wa taṭhīr al-a'rāq*. Cairo: Maṭb'at Muḥammad 'Alī Ṣubayḥ, 1959.

—. *Tajārib al-umam*. The concluding portion, edited by H. F. Amedroz as Vols I and II of *The Eclipse of the Abbasid Caliphate*. Cairo: Maṭba'at sharikat al-Tamaddun al-Sinā'iyya, AH 1333 (AD 1915).

fl. 985 al Muqaddasī, 'Abd Allāh Muḥammad ibn Aḥmad. *Aḥsan al-tāqāsīm fī ma'rifat al-aqālīm*. Leiden, 1877.

al-Murtaḍā. See Ibn al-Murtaḍā.

877 Muslim ibn al-Ḥajjāj. *Ṣaḥīḥ*. Cairo: Muḥammad Ṣubayḥ.

Early 19th century **Najāt al-umma fī tā'at al-a'imma*. Princeton, Yehuda Collection, MS No. 4275.

Late 19th century *al-Naqshabandī, Aḥmad ibn Da'ūd. *Hidāyat al-hunafā ilā ṭā'at al-khulafā'*. Princeton, Yehuda Collection MS No. 3203.

1311 al-Nasafī, 'Umar ibn Muḥammad. *al-'Aqā'id*. Sharḥ al-Taftāzānī. Istanbul, 1891.

fl. 880s [Pseudo-] Nawbakhtī, Abū Muḥammad al-Ḥasan ibn Mūsā. *Fīraq al-Shī'a*. Edited by Muḥammad Ṣādiq Āl Baḥr al-'Ulūm. Najaf: al-Maktaba al-Murtaḍawiyya, 1936.

Nemoy, Leon. *Arabic Manuscripts in the Yale University Library*. (Vol. 40 of the Translations of the Connecticut Academy of Arts and Sciences.) New Haven: Connecticut Academy of Arts and Sciences, 1956.

1092 Niẓām al-Mulk, Abū 'Alī al-Ḥasan. *Siyāsatnāma*. Translated from Persian into English by Hubert Darke under the title *The Book of Government*. London: Routledge and Kegan Paul, 1960.

al-Nu'mān. See al-Qāḍī al-Nu'mān.

1332 al-Nuwayrī, Shihāb al-Dīn Aḥmad ibn 'Abd al-Wahhāb. *Nihāyat al-arab fī funūn al-adab*. Cairo: Dār al-Kutub, 1926.

Plessner, M. *Der Oikonomikos des Neupythagoräres Bryson*. Heidelberg, 1928.

974 al-Qāḍī al-Nu'mān ibn Muḥammad al-Maghribī. *Da'ā'im al-Islām*. Edited by A. A. A. Fyzee. Cairo: Dār al-Ma'ārif, Vol. I (1951), Vol. II (1960).

—. *Kitāb al-himma fī ādāb atbā' al-a'imma*. Edited by Muḥammad Kāmil Ḥusayn. Cairo: Dār al-Fikr al-'Arabī, n.d.

1418 al-Qalqashandī, Abū al-'Abbās Aḥmad. *Ṣubḥ al-a'shā fī ṣinā'at al-inshā*. Cairo: al-Maṭba'a al-Amīriyya. 1913.

1517 al-Qastalānī, Aḥmad ibn Muḥammad. *Irshād al-sārī li-sharḥ ṣaḥīḥ al-Bukhārī*. Cairo: Bulaq, AH 1305 (AD 1887).

al-Qur'ān. Cairo: al-Maṭba'a al-amīriyya, AH 1376 (AD 1956).

1072 al-Qushayrī, Abū al-Qāsim 'Abd al-Karīm. *al-Risāla al-Qushayriyya*. Cairo: Muṣṭafā al-Bābī al-Ḥalabī, 1959.

al-Rayyis, Muḥammad Ḍiyā' al- Dīn. *al-Naẓarāt al-siyāsiyya al-islāmiyya*. Cairo: Maktabat al-Anglo al-Miṣriyya, 1960.

Riḍā, Muḥammad Rashīd. *al-Khilāfa aw al-imāma al-'uẓmā*. Cairo: Maṭba'at al-Manār, AH 1341 (AD 1922).

—. *Tafsīr al-Manār*. Cairo: Matba'at Muḥammad 'Ali Ṣubayḥ, AH 1374 (AD 1954).

Rosenthal, E. I. J. *Political Thought in Medieval Islam*. Cambridge: University Press, 1958.

Rosenthal, F. 'State and religion according to Abū al-Ḥasan al-'Āmirī', *Islamic Quarterly*, III (1956).

1056 al-Ṣābī, Abū al-Ḥusayn Hilāl. *Ta'rīkh*. Vol. VIII edited by H. F. Amedroz and D. S. Margoliouth and published in Vol. III of *The Eclipse of the Abbasid Caliphate*. Cairo: Matba'at Sharikat al-Tamaddun al-Ṣinā'iyya, AH 1337 (AD 1919).

1497 al-Sakhāwī, Shams al-Dīn Muḥammad ibn 'Abd al-Raḥmān. *al-I'lān bi al-tawbīkh liman dhamma al-ta'rīkh*. Damascus: Maṭba'at al-taraqqī, AH 1349 (AD 1931).

1164 al-Sam'ānī, 'Abd al-Karīm Abū Sa'īd ibn Muḥammad. *Kitāb al-ansāb*. (E. J. W. Memorial, 20) Leiden, 1912.

Sayyid, Fu'ād. 'Makhṭuṭāt al-Yaman', *Majallat Ma'had al-Makhṭūṭāt al-'Arabiyya*, Vol. I, 1955.

1153 al-Shahrastanī, Muḥammad ibn ʿAbd al-Karīm. *al-Milal wa al-niḥal*. Edited by Muḥammad Kīlānī. Cairo: Muṣṭafā Babī al-Ḥalabī, 1961.

—. *Nihāyat al-iqdām fī ʿilm al-kalām*. Edited and translated by A. Guillaume. Oxford University Press, 1934.

Sharḥ al-Maqāṣid [fī ʿilm al-kalām, by Saʿd al-Dīn ʿUmar al-Taftāzānī]. Istanbul, AH 1305 (AD 1887).

fl. late 11th c. [al-Shayzarī], ʿAbd al-Raḥmān. *al-Manhaj al-maslūk fī siyāsat al-mulūk*. Cairo: Maṭbaʿat al-Ẓāhir, AH 1326 (AD 1908).

al-Shayzarī, ʿAbd al-Raḥmān. *Nihāyat al-rutba fī ṭalab al-ḥisba*. Cairo: Lajnat al-Ta'līf wa al-Tarjama wa al-Nashr, 1946.

1084 al-Shīrāzī, Abū Isḥāq Ibrāhīm ibn ʿAlī. *Ṭabaqāt al-fuqahā'*, Baghdad, AH 1356 (AD 1937).

1370 al-Subkī, Tāj al-dīn ʿAbd al-Wahhāb ibn ʿAlī. *Muʿīd al-niʿam wa mubīd al-niqam*. Edited by Muḥammad ʿAlī al-Najjār et al. Cairo: Jamāʿat al-Azhar li-al-Nashr wa al-Ta'līf, 1948.

—. *Tabaqāt al-Shāfiʿiyya al-kubrā*. Cairo: al-Maṭbaʿa al-Ḥusayniyya al-Miṣriyya, AH 1324 (AD 1906).

1505 al-Suyūtī, ʿAbd al-Raḥmān ibn Abī Bakr. *al-Durr al-manthūr fī al-tafsīr bil-ma'thūr*. Tehran, AH 1377 (AD 1957).

—. *al-Itqān fī ʿulūm al-Qur'ān*. Cairo: Maṭbaʿat al-Maʿāhid, Maktabat Maḥmūd Tawfīq, AH 1354 (AD 1935).

923 al-Ṭabarī, Muḥammad ibn Jarīr. *Tafsīr al-Qur'ān*. Cairo: Dār al-Maʿārif.

—. *Ta'rīkh al-rusul wa al-mulūk*. Cairo: Dār al-Maʿārif, 1960.

1390 al-Taftāzānī, Saʿd al-Dīn ʿUmar. See *Sharḥ al-Maqāṣid*.

1555 Ṭāshköprüzade, Ahmad ibn Muṣṭafā. *Kitāb miftāh al-saʿāda wa miṣbāḥ al-siyāda*. Hyderabad: Dā'irat al-Maʿārif, AH 1329–56 (AD 1911–37).

1023 al-Tawḥīdī, Abū Ḥayyān. *al-Imtāʿ wa al-mu'ānasa*. 3 vols. Edited by Ziriklī. Cairo: Maṭbaʿat Lajnat al-Ta'līf wa al-Tarjama wa al-Nashr, 1953.

1038 al-Thaʿālibī, Abū Manṣūr ʿAbd al-Malik. *Yatīmat al-dahr fī maḥāsin ahl al-ʿasr*. Cairo: Matbaʿat al-Saʿāda, al maktaba al-Tijāriyya, AH 1375–7 (AD 1956–8).

c. 1126 al-Ṭurṭūshī, Abū Bakr Muḥammad. *Sirāj al-mulūk*. Cairo: al-Maṭbaʿa al-maḥmūdiyya al-Tijāriyya, AH 1354 (AH 1935).

Ullmann Walter. *Principles of Government and Politics in the Middle Ages*. London: Methuen, 1961.

Wensinck, A. J. 'Les preuves de l'existence de Dieu dans la théologie musulmane', *Koninklijke Akademie van Wetenschappen*, Vol. 81 (1936–7) Ser. A. No. 2.

Wittek, Paul. *The Rise of the Ottoman Empire*. London: Royal Asiatic Society, 1965.

1367 al-Yāfiʿī, Abū Muḥammad ʿAbd Allāh ibn Asʿad. *Mir'āt al-janān wa ʿibrat al-yaqẓān*. Hyderabad: Maṭbaʿat Dā'irat al-Maʿārif, AH 1337 (AD 1919).

1229 Yāqūt, Shihāb al-Dīn Abū ʿAbd Allāh ibn ʿAbd Allāh. *Kitāb Irshād al-arīb ilā maʿrifat al-adīb*. Edited by D. S. Margoliouth. Cairo: Maṭbaʿat Hindiyya, 1907–26.

1144 al-Zamakhsharī, Maḥmūd ibn ʿUmar. *al-Kashshāf*. Cairo: al-Maktaba al-Tijāriyya, 1953.

al-Zaydān, Jurjī. *Ta'rīkh ādāb al-lugha al-'Arabiyya*. Vol. II. Cairo, 1912.
al-Ziriklī, Khayr al-Dīn. *al-A'lām*. Cairo: al-Maṭba'a al-'Arabiyya, 1927–8.

Index